WE BOTH READ®

Picture Puzzles

Acertijos con imágenes

By Sindy McKay

TREASURE BAY

Parent's Introduction

We Both Read books have been developed by reading specialists to invite parents and children to interact as they read together. This particular book is designed for a parent or adult to read the entire book to a child. However, throughout the book the child is invited to actively participate by looking at the pictures and responding to questions.

In this book, you read the question on the right-hand page. Then, before turning the page, your child tries to guess the answer. When you turn the page, the left-hand page shows the answer.

Consider encouraging children to think of this as a game or puzzle, which they can solve by looking at and thinking about the pictures. If needed, you can provide support by helping to identify what is in the pictures and asking what is the same or different about them. In some cases you may be able to eliminate some pictures as you discuss what might be the correct answer.

Reading this book together will assist in the development of cognitive thinking and learning skills that will help your child in school. Depending upon your child, it may be helpful to read only a part of the book at a time. Most of all, remember to praise your child's efforts and keep the interaction fun.

Introducción para los padres

Los libros de We Both Read han sido desarrollados por especialistas en lectura para que los padres y los niños interactúen mientras leen juntos. Este libro en particular está diseñado para que uno de los padres o un adulto le lea el libro completo al niño. Sin embargo, durante todo el libro se invita al niño a participar mientras mira las imágenes y responde a las preguntas.

En este libro, se leen las preguntas que aparecen en la página derecha. Después, antes de pasar la página, el niño intenta adivinar la respuesta. Cuando pasa la página, la respuesta aparece en la página izquierda.

Es bueno animar a los niños para que piensen que esto es un juego o un rompecabezas que pueden resolver mirando las imágenes y reflexionando acerca de ellas. Si es necesario, puede ayudar al niño a identificar las imágenes preguntando cuáles son las similitudes y las diferencias entre ellas. En algunos casos, se pueden ir eliminando imágenes a la vez que se conversa acerca de cuál puede ser la respuesta correcta.

Leer este libro juntos fomentará el desarrollo del pensamiento cognitivo y de las habilidades de aprendizaje que ayudarán al niño en la escuela. Dependiendo del niño, puede que sea beneficioso leer solo una parte del libro a la vez. Lo más importante es que elogie los esfuerzos del niño y que la interacción entre los dos siempre sea divertida.

Picture Puzzles
Acertijos con imágenes

A We Both Read® Book
Bilingual in English and Spanish
Level PK-K
Guided Reading: Level AA

English text copyright © 2022 by Sindy McKay
Bilingual adaptation and Spanish text © 2023 by Treasure Bay, Inc.
Use of photographs provided by iStock and Dreamstime.

We Both Read® is a trademark of Treasure Bay, Inc.

All rights reserved.

Published by
Treasure Bay, Inc.
PO Box 519
Roseville, CA 95661 USA

Library of Congress Control Number: 2022942074

Printed in South Korea

ISBN: 978-1-60115-051-6

Visit us online at:
WeBothRead.com

PR-10-22

Which animal does not belong on a farm?

¿Qué animal no pertenece a una granja?

The lion.

A lion is much more at home on the plains of Africa than on a farm. Lions hunt during the night and spend most of their days resting.

El león.

El león está mucho más a gusto en las llanuras de África que en una granja. Los leones cazan durante la noche y pasan la mayor parte del día descansando.

Which child is eating fruit?

¿Cuál de los niños está comiendo fruta?

This child is eating an apple, which is a type of fruit.

What kinds of food are the other children eating?

———— ◆ ————

Este niño está comiendo una manzana, que es un tipo de fruta.

¿Qué tipo de comida están comiendo los otros niños?

Hot dog
Perrito caliente

Cereal
Cereal

Carrot
Zanahoria

Which one can run the fastest?

———◆———

¿Cuál es el que corre más rápido?

The horse.

There was one horse that was able to run fifty-five miles per hour. That's as fast as some cars go on the highway. That's a lot faster than turtles, snails, or humans can run!

---◆---

El caballo.

Había un caballo que era capaz de correr a cincuenta y cinco millas por hora. Así de rápido van algunos autos en la autopista. Es mucho más rápido de lo que pueden correr las tortugas, los caracoles o los humanos.

Which building is the tallest?

¿Qué edificio es el más alto?

The skyscraper.

The tallest skyscraper in the world is more than a half-mile high.

◆

El rascacielos.

El rascacielos más alto del mundo tiene más de media milla de altura.

Which one is not like the others?

¿Cuál no es como los demás?

The flower.

The other pictures are all of animals. Can you think of what is different between a flower or a plant and animals?

———◆———

La flor.

Las otras imágenes son todos de animales. ¿Puedes pensar en qué se diferencia una flor o una planta de los animales?

Lemur   **Chameleon**   **Dog**
Lémur   *Camaleón*   *Perro*

Which one has the smallest feet?

---◆---

¿Cuál tiene los pies más pequeños?

11

The mouse.

Did you know that elephants can "hear" with their feet? Their feet can feel the low rumbles of other elephants up to twenty miles away!

---◆---

El ratón.

¿Sabías que los elefantes pueden "oír" con sus pies? ¡Los pies pueden sentir los sonidos graves de otros elefantes hasta a veinte millas de distancia!

Which one does **not** belong at a picnic?

---◆---

¿Cuál **no** pertenece a un pícnic?

13

The couch.

Picnics are fun! But why are there always so many ants at a picnic? First, a few ants may visit your picnic to enjoy the food. When those ants return to the nest, they leave a scent trail for all their ant friends to follow back to your picnic!

◆

El sofá.

¡Los pícnics son divertidos! Pero ¿por qué siempre hay tantas hormigas en un pícnic? Primero, algunas hormigas pueden visitar tu pícnic para disfrutar de la comida. Cuando esas hormigas vuelven al nido, ¡dejan un rastro de olor para que todas sus amigas hormigas lo sigan hasta tu pícnic!

Which animal would make a good house pet?

———◆———

¿Qué animal sería una buena mascota para una casa?

The hamster.

Hamsters make great pets! Unfortunately, lots of interesting animals, like gorillas, penguins, and octopuses, wouldn't be good as pets. Can you think of any reasons why?

---◆---

El hámster.

¡Los hámsteres son buenas mascotas! Por desgracia, muchos animales interesantes, como los gorilas, los pingüinos y los pulpos, no serían buenos como mascotas. ¿Se te ocurre alguna razón para eso?

Gorilla
Gorila

Penguin
Pingüino

Octopus
Pulpo

Which item might you use on a rainy day?

◆

¿Qué objeto podrías utilizar en un día de lluvia?

The umbrella.

You might want an umbella on a rainy day.

When do you think you might use these other things?

---◆---

El paraguas.

Es posible que quieras un paraguas en un día de lluvia.

¿Cuándo crees que podrías utilizar estas otras cosas?

Which one is a different kind of animal?

---◆---

¿Cuál de los animales es de un tipo diferente?

19

The lizard.

This green basilisk lizard is a type of reptile. It doesn't fly. The other animals are all birds that fly.

Flamingos can often be seen standing in the water on one leg, but they can also fly very fast for long distances.

◆

El lagarto.

Este lagarto basilisco verde es un tipo de reptil. No vuela. Los otros animales son todos pájaros que vuelan.

Los flamencos suelen verse de pie en el agua sobre una pata, pero también pueden volar muy rápido durante largas distancias.

Which one is not like the others?

───◆───

¿Cuál no se parece a los demás?

21

The airplane.

An airplane travels through the air. The sailboat, speedboat and canoe, all travel on water.

---◆---

El avión.

El avión viaja por el aire. El velero, la lancha y la canoa viajan por el agua.

Sailboat
Velero

Speedboat
Lancha rápida

Canoe
Canoa

Which animal has spots?

◆

¿Qué animal tiene manchas?

The cheetah.

The zebra has stripes. Did you know that no two zebras have stripes that look exactly the same?

---◆---

El guepardo.

La cebra tiene rayas. ¿Sabías que no hay dos cebras que tengan rayas exactamente iguales?

Which two items would you find on a soccer field?

―――――◆―――――

¿Qué dos objetos encontrarías en una cancha de fútbol?

25

The soccer ball and net.

You don't usually see a sack of potatoes or a pair of monkeys at a soccer game.

◆

La pelota de fútbol y la red.

No es común ver una bolsa de papas o un par de monos en un partido de fútbol.

Which picture is showing a different season than the others?

◆

¿Qué imagen muestra una estación diferente a las demás?

The children jumping in the water.

These kids are having fun in the summer season! The pictures with snow were taken in the winter. When snow melts in the spring, it becomes water that flows into rivers and lakes.

---◆---

Los niños que saltan al agua.

¡Estos niños se divierten en la estación de verano! Las fotos con nieve se tomaron en invierno. Cuando la nieve se derrite en primavera, se convierte en agua que fluye hacia los ríos y lagos.

Which of these would you probably not see in a park?

◆

¿Cuál de estas cosas no sería probable ver en un parque?

29

The bed.

Beds are usually found in bedrooms. However, if you were in a park you might find a flower bed.

---◆---

La cama.

Las camas suelen encontrarse en los dormitorios. Sin embargo, si estuvieras en un parque podrías encontrar un sector con muchas flores. ¡Este tiene forma de cama!

Which vehicle do firefighters use?

◆

¿Qué vehículo utilizan los bomberos?

The fire truck or fire engine.

After working hard all day, firefighters might enjoy getting ice cream from an ice cream truck! And when they get home they might get mail that was delivered by someone using a mail truck.

──────── ◆ ────────

El camión de bomberos o autobomba.

Después de trabajar duro todo el día, puede que los bomberos quieran disfrutar de un helado de un camión de helados. Y cuando lleguen a casa puede que reciban el correo que les ha entregado alguien con un camión de correos.

Ice cream truck
Camión de helados

Mail truck
Camión de correos

Which musical instrument is not like the others?

¿Qué instrumento musical no es como los demás?

The violin.

The violin is a string instrument. You play it by drawing a bow across the strings. The trombone, trumpet, and tuba are brass instruments. You play them by blowing into them.

---◆---

El violín.

El violín es un instrumento de cuerda. Se toca pasando un arco por las cuerdas. El trombón, la trompeta y la tuba son instrumentos de metal. Se tocan soplando dentro de ellos.

Trombone	Trumpet	Tuba
Trombón	*Trompeta*	*Tuba*

Which vehicle has the most wheels?

―――――――◆―――――――

¿Qué vehículo tiene más ruedas?

This vehicle has the most wheels.

How many wheels do you think it has? (Remember to count the wheels you cannot see on the other side!)

--- ◆ ---

Este vehículo es el que tiene más ruedas.

¿Cuántas ruedas crees que tiene? (¡recuerda contar las ruedas que no puedes ver en el otro lado!)

Three wheels
Tres ruedas

Four wheels
Cuatro ruedas

Which tool would you not use to build a house?

¿Qué herramienta no utilizarías para construir una casa?

The hair dryer.

A hair dryer might be helpful after the workers take a shower, but it won't help them build the house!

These items are much more helpful!

El secador de pelo.

Un secador de pelo puede ser útil después de que los trabajadores se duchen, ¡pero no les ayudará a construir la casa!

¡Estos objetos son mucho más útiles!

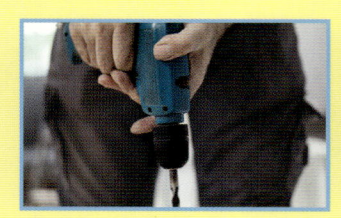

Saw	Drill	Hammer
Sierra	*Taladro*	*Martillo*

Which one is not like the others?

¿Cuál no es como los demás?

39

The car.

The car has four wheels. The bicycles have two wheels.

Remember to wear your helmet!

———————◆———————

El auto.

El auto tiene cuatro ruedas. Las bicicletas tienen dos ruedas.

¡Recuerda ponerte el casco!

Which animal is the shortest?

———◆———

¿Qué animal es más bajito?

The dog.

The smallest dog on record was a Chihuahua (chee-WOW-wah) named Milly, who was only four inches tall. That's shorter than a can of soda! The tallest giraffe was about nineteen feet tall. That's as tall as a two-story house!

———— ◆ ————

El perro.

El perro más pequeño del que se tiene constancia era una chihuahua llamada Milly, que solo medía cuatro pulgadas. ¡Menos que una lata de refresco! La jirafa más alta medía unos diecinueve pies. ¡Tan alta como una casa de dos pisos!

Alpaca Giraffe Pony
Alpaca *Jirafa* *Poni*

If you liked **Picture Puzzles**, here are some other We Both Read® books you are sure to enjoy!

*Si te gustaron los **Acertijos con imágenes**, ¡aquí tienes otros libros de We Both Read® que seguro que te gustarán!*

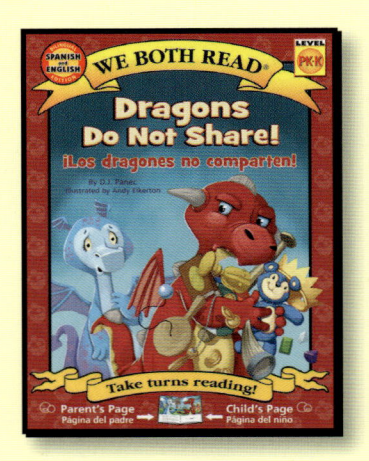

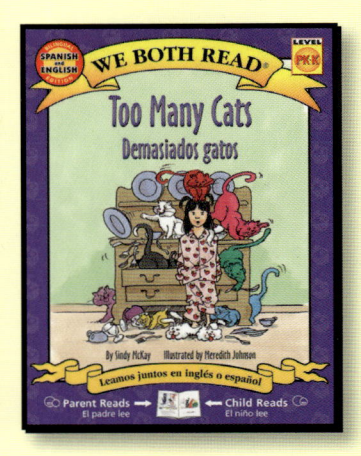

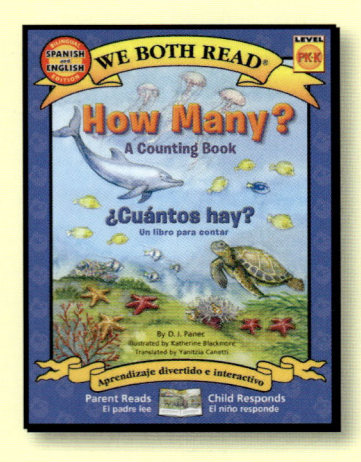

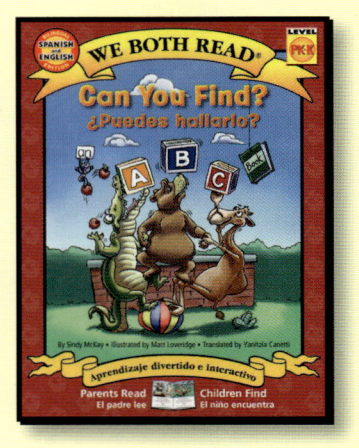

To see all the We Both Read books that are available, just go online to **WeBothRead.com**.

*Para ver todos los libros de We Both Read que están disponibles, solo tienes que visitar la página web **WeBothRead.com**.*

JERRY C. DAVIS

REHABBING FOR PROFIT

McGRAW-HILL BOOK COMPANY
New York   St. Louis   San Francisco   Auckland
Bogotá   Hamburg   Johannesburg   London   Madrid   Mexico
Montreal   New Delhi   Panama   Paris   São Paulo
Singapore   Sydney   Tokyo   Toronto

Library of Congress Cataloging in Publication Data

Davis, Jerry C
  Rehabbing for profit.

Includes index.
1. Housing rehabilitation–United States.
2. Real estate investment–United States.
I. Title.
HD7293.D32   332.63'243   80-16357
ISBN 0-07-015695-6

Copyright © 1981 by McGraw-Hill, Inc. All rights reserved. Printed in the United States of America. No part of this publication may be reproduced, stored in a retrieval system, or transmitted, in any form or by any means, electronic, mechanical, photocopying, recording, or otherwise, without the prior written permission of the publisher.

234567890 KPKP 8987654321

The editors for this book were Jeremy Robinson and Christine M. Ulwick, the designer was Elliot Epstein, and the production supervisor was Sally Fliess. It was set in Baskerville by Datapage.

Printed and bound by Kingsport Press.

CONTENTS

	Preface	vii
1	WHAT SHOULD YOU BUY?	1
2	CHOOSING THE PROPERTY	9
3	HOW MUCH IS IT WORTH?	29
4	BUYING IT FOR LESS	51
5	HOW DO YOU FINANCE IT?	59
6	FINDING LABOR FOR THE JOB	87
7	BUILDING PERMITS AND INSPECTIONS	99
8	MAKING COSMETIC IMPROVEMENTS	103
9	REHAB INVOLVING CONSTRUCTION	115
10	RENTING FOR PROFIT	135
11	SELLING FOR PROFIT	151
12	CONVERTING TO CONDOMINIUM OWNERSHIP	161
	Glossary	169
	Index	175

PREFACE

The profit motive undoubtedly ranks as the primary reason why people buy buildings to rehabilitate them. But, many of those who have completed successful rehab projects speak about additional satisfactions they have received beyond the monetary rewards.

To take something ugly and decayed and make it attractive and contemporary apparently provides an additional return beyond the bottom line of the financial statement. For one thing, a rehab project can engage a participant's sense of creativity and imagination. It is not like other investments in that sense. There is some pleasure in seeing the end result when a building is reborn.

There is also the matter of taking part in the process personally. The greatest benefits in a rehab project go to those who can handle as much of the work as possible with their own hands and skills. Nothing seems to please a rehabber more than to strip the cover of a wall or fireplace and find something special behind it.

Finally, there is the pleasure of helping to restore a building that is part of a general revitalization of a neighborhood. On a block where the rehabilitation of several buildings is underway simultaneously, there is a spirit of common interest and appreciation for each other's efforts, which is rarely observed in an investment situation.

It is the assumption of this book, however, that all of those emotions are secondary to this question: Will the property that is created by the rehabilitation cover all the costs of the job and return a respectable profit for the effort?

In a great many cases—by far the majority—rehabilitation has proven to be a profitable investment. It has been the route into real estate investment for thousands of people who had no particular knowledge of the field or special manual skills. In many instances, they also had very little capital.

Predicting what an investor will realize from a rehab project is much more difficult than for a new building. There are many more variable factors in a rehab. Will the neighborhood rebound and grow in demand? Will the cost of the job coincide with initial estimates? Will tenants be willing to pay the higher rents that the investor expects from a rehabbed building?

All of these factors are *not* concerns of the buyer of a building that needs no work in a neighborhood where people already have shown they want to live and where rents reflect that demand. On the other hand, buildings that need no rehab work often return little income to their owners because they are expensive to buy. The rents cover the mortgage payments and the expenses in these buildings, and that is about it.

The buildings rehabbers like are those they can buy at a low price because the property is old and run-down, improve with their own efforts or those of labor that might be purchased inexpensively, and then sell or rent to most profitable advantage. Often, the return on these properties is much greater than that from the newer buildings.

Older buildings are less expensive to buy for another good reason, besides the fact that they are old. They were built at a time when materials and labor cost a fraction of what they do today. The owner who is selling to a rehabber may still be thinking in terms of what was originally paid for the building and be out of touch with what has been happening in the real estate market just enough that, even for a neglected property, the price is a bargain.

Surprisingly, a strong interest in the rehabilitation of buildings exists in all areas of the country, not just in the older cities. Even in such relatively new cities as Dallas, Houston, and San Francisco, many buildings are sick, but not terminal. Where these buildings have declined, small investors have often been there to turn them around and try to make some money from the deal.

The most common rehab strategy has been to improve a building, rent the units (except, perhaps, for one that the investor will occupy) for a few years until the property appreciates still more in value, and then sell, trade, or refinance it.

Other rehabbers choose to improve a residential unit that they intend to use for themselves. They are content to gradually upgrade the property—usually a house, but sometimes the best apartment in a multiunit building—until a good opportunity comes along to sell and buy something else.

The rationale for choosing only to rehab a home intended for personal occupancy can be as persuasively argued as that for buying a building with several units. It is as near to being a risk-free investment as one can find and has had an uninterrupted ascendance in value since World War II.

Rental units also have had strong demand, especially in the last 3 years, when so few new apartment properties have been developed. However, the investor in rental property has had to cope with increasingly higher expenses, especially in energy costs. Those who did not or could not raise rents enough to cover those costs got caught in a squeeze, and some suffered actual cash losses (though partially recovered through tax advantages).

The multiunit rental project offers tax benefits that the owner-occupied house does not enjoy in that an additional income tax deduction can be claimed for depreciation.

Actually, all real estate enjoys special tax advantages. For example, any payment of interest on a mortgage or on money borrowed for a rehabilitation job is deductible. In fact, the materials themselves are deductible, as well as any labor used on the job, in most cases. So is property tax. Then, when the property is sold, it receives the favored capital gains treatment on any profits. If exchanged or refinanced, there is no tax of any kind—until an eventual sale occurs.

It is government policy in this country to help people own real estate, so the government does a lot of things to help them. For example, it insures or directly loans money at low interest. It also makes improvements that increase the value of property. The government may build sidewalks or roads to the property, increase public services, provide better transit service, and offer general programs for entire neighborhood revitalization.

Another friend of the rehabber is the mortgage lender. Financial institutions want to see the property near their offices or in the cities they serve upgraded, not in decline. That is why one of the first sources to talk to about a rehabilitation plan is the mortgage lender nearest to the property. The neighborhood lending institution has the most at stake in seeing that its office does not end up in the center of a slum, with nobody to make deposits and nobody to borrow money.

Perhaps the person that most needs to be convinced that the concept of improving a building makes sense is the investor. It is no easy route to wealth. When a building really needs work, it can be a long and tedious job that may be more expensive than it looks. While this book will attempt to deal with the known problems to be encountered, there is the unknown of *the investor's commitment.* If you want an easy investment, buy a bond. Consider, however, that a successful rehab effort may be difficult, but it should pay much more than a bond. It has for many who have tried it.

Typically, the newcomer to rehab buys a small multiunit building; does most of the labor, perhaps assisted by friends; then moves into one unit and rents the other(s). The rent from the tenants covers some, but not all, of the mortgage payments and expenses. To the extent that someone is helping the owner make mortgage payments, the shelter costs to the investor are reduced. Furthermore, the owner of the building takes a tax shelter that tenants do not enjoy.

Eventually, the investor wants a large enough building that the rents will cover all of the mortgage costs and put some dollars in the pocket. The typical strategy to achieve that goal works like this:

Rehab one building; get it filled with tenants paying substantially more than the building previously produced in income. Then sell it, pay off the mortgage, and use the combined equity and appreciation as downpayment on a larger building.

That scenario has been repeated time and again by investors who moved to bigger and bigger properties, seeking both more income and faster growth in wealth.

The investor then gets the idea of buying two buildings or maybe trading the building for two others. Now the investor can afford buildings that need little or no rehab work. The tax shelter is substantial, and the income is flowing well. The investor can turn to professional management to handle the maintenance. The next step in many cases has been for the investor to quit a presently held job and devote all time and attention to real estate.

That is the ideal. The reverse of that is when an investor gets in too deep, tries to tackle a job that is too expensive or difficult, gets discouraged, and walks away from the investment. The investor also may find something incurable or beyond current ability to finance. Or, worst of all, the building may be the only one upgraded in a dying neighborhood, and the investor may be left with a high-rent property in a low-rent location.

Every investment has its dangers. It is necessary to weigh the potential rewards against the risks. Carefully considered rehabilitation projects usually fulfill their objectives. It is to offer the best advice of those who have successfully produced many rehabilitated buildings that this book will be concerned.

Jerry C. Davis

1 WHAT SHOULD YOU BUY?

At least a half dozen ways to rehab for profit are available to investors. The type you choose depends on such circumstances as these:

- Whether you want to live in the building after it is rehabbed.
- Whether you are willing to take on the management and maintenance chores of the building.
- Whether you intend to hold the property and rent it out, or try to sell it for an immediate profit after it has been rehabbed.
- How much of your own time and effort you are willing to put into the rehab job.
- Whether you would rather start with one unit—a house—or try a multiunit building.
- How big a building you want to tackle.
- Whether you can afford what it takes to improve a building to the point that people might want to buy the units as part of a condominium conversion.

Each of these points should be weighed seriously. If you are buying in an area that looks safe enough to live in, you might want to occupy a unit (or a house, if you prefer the single-unit alternative), until the neighborhood completes its turnaround. Then, the profits from the rehab will be much greater than if you rehab and sell immediately.

This especially is true if you manage and maintain the building yourself. This means you handle routine maintenance, keep up the yard, deal with complaints, perform whatever services the building needs (vacuuming the hallways and stairs, raking the leaves, shoveling the snow), and otherwise serve as a janitor-in-residence.

Being a janitor-in-residence is not all bad. Rehabbers estimate it is worth 10 to 15 percent of the expenses of running the building. That is money in your pocket instead of someone else's.

Living in the building has the advantage that the rent you would pay to another landlord is paid to yourself. At least, some of it is. In a two- or three-flat, you cannot expect rents from tenants to cover all mortgage payments, taxes, repairs, and other expenses. Sometimes, with four units—usually with more—all those expenses are covered and the owner nets some cash. At least your costs of occupancy are much reduced by the fact that you are sharing the expenses of ownership of real estate with other people and taking the tax benefits they do not receive.

Some rehab investors do not want to get involved with tenants in any way. They just want to buy a property cheap, do the work, and get rid of it at a substantially higher dollar to somebody else. That is fine, except that it is hard work to produce a rehab project, and it may be more time-consuming than it is worth, unless the building is held for a while to gain some additional appreciation.

True, any pumpkin that is turned into a coach is going to be more valuable immediately. However, when favorable trends are developing in an area but have not yet fully materialized, it pays to hold onto the property and await the higher demand. Real estate is not like the stock market, where it is never considered a mistake to take a good profit. The likelihood that more profit lies ahead for the patient investor is much more assured on a real estate investment than a portfolio of stocks.

Conversion of a small building to condominium ownership holds out intriguing possibilities to the investor who does not want tenant worries. When you are rehabbing for people who are going to buy rather than rent your units, however, the rehab job must be done with extra quality that may be expensive.

Buildings with as few as three units have been converted successfully from rental to condominium status. Such conversion can produce a windfall for the converter. If the property is divided into several units and each of them is sold, the value of the parts somehow exceeds the value of the whole—often by a great deal. That is, the owner can sell three units for $50,000 each, or $150,000 added together, while the building as a three-unit rental property would be tied to the amount of income it produced and might sell for only $100,000 on that basis. (Condominium conversion is both so attractive and so different from other rehab opportunities that it will be covered in a separate chapter of this book.)

Finally, before beginning any rehab effort, the investor must consider the limits of personal time that can be committed to the actual work on the property. That factor dominates everything from what to buy to begin with, to how much the job will cost, to how to get the job done.

WHAT SHOULD YOU BUY? 3

Figure 1–1 Consider your own abilities and available time for rehab work because your commitment can make the investment work.

For example, if you are going to turn the whole thing over to a contractor and can afford it, you might consider buying a building that has to be completely gutted. The building is cheapest that is obviously the most difficult to salvage, and one that has to be gutted should be the least expensive to buy. There is a very limited market for people who want to go that far with a building, so plenty of real-eyesore buildings are available if you have the nerve.

If you expect to do as much of the work as possible to save on rehab costs, then you look for a building that has few, if any, major problems, one that responds well to simple cosmetic treatment, such as painting, scraping, sanding, and wallpapering.

Many investors look for a building in the way former government worker, now full-time rehabber Richard Falstein goes about it. According to him:

> The big factor for us is that the building have charm potential after it is rehabbed. My wife is particularly talented at perceiving what a building will be like after it is renovated. We look for high ceilings, hidden parlor doors, hardwood floors—things like that. We never gut a building. We may

knock down a few walls to improve room sizes, but mostly we try to restore the innate charm.

In addition to how energetic you are to do your own rehab and maintenance, your self-analysis should take into account how nervous you are about your investments. The types of investment available to a rehabber vary in degree of risk. Here is how they line up:

The least risky investment is the house in a good neighborhood that has not been maintained as well as other properties. It is set amid sound, attractive homes, but has been allowed to take on a run-down look that is atypical of the area. This type property turns up rather frequently and can be highly rewarding if uncovered and bought inexpensively.

If this kind of investment appeals to you, tell real estate brokers about your interest. In the course of looking at each property that sales personnel have listed, brokers see a number of "dogs" that are well-located, but look as if they will be hard to sell because they are so poorly maintained. Maybe the owner did not have the money or the inclination to keep up with the neighbors as they added things to their homes to make them more valuable. So, now there is an ugly $35,000 house sitting in a block with spruce-looking homes that would easily command $45,000.

When you tour such a home, let your imagination run loose as to what might be changed and upgraded. Would new shutters, a row of shrubs around the front yard, or a different color for the exterior improve its appearance from the outside? Could small rooms be combined, the kitchen modernized, or a bath added to bring it up to its neighbors' interiors?

If your own imagination is limited, take an interior designer along. You will have as many ideas as you can handle from that source.

The important point to remember is not to get carried away. Spending $5000 or even $7000 to make a $35,000 house as desirable as its $45,000 neighbors is a good investment. But, spending $15,000 makes no economic sense.

This kind of house usually will be easy to finance because the lender knows the neighborhood is solid. The money to refurbish it can be borrowed separately or as part of the first mortgage.

The reason the property is so risk-free (if structural soundness and no unexpected problems of a major order are assumed) is that it will rise in value as the neighborhood does, even if it is just maintained in a reasonable way and not allowed to go completely to pot. Neighborhoods tend to appreciate as a unit, especially individual blocks of neighborhoods. Thus, as property values increase around a run-down house, even the run-down house draws some benefits from the trend.

As safe, but not usually as profitable, an investment is a house that a rehabber intends to occupy personally. This form of rehab also offers great opportunity for self-expression. The owner-occupant can do it slowly, one room at a time, as money becomes available. (However, it should be borne in mind that, if you do it that way instead of all at once before move-in, you will be living in a construction zone for a long time, with all the inconvenience that implies.)

The maintenance costs will be rock-bottom because you will be handling it yourself. Financing will be easy to obtain because the buyer will be the occupant. Because it is a single-family house, it will appreciate at least as fast as multiunit buildings when the neighborhood improves.

A drawback to be considered is that the neighborhood still might not be one in which you or your family would feel safe. To await the full turnaround of the area, you might prefer to rent it. In that case, though, the rehab work would have to be done upfront, not over a period of months or years, as would be possible if you were the occupant.

Moreover, your profit would be well down the road. It would not be bankable until you sold the property. (An exception to that statement would be if the neighborhood improved so rapidly that values really soared. Then, it would be smart to consider refinancing and taking some of the profit out to invest in another building.)

The next-safest investment would be a house rehabbed for rental in an area that already shows definite and unmistakable signs of revival. If the tenant is chosen carefully, you will have occupants who will tend to regard the house almost as their own. You can even make arrangements that, as part of the lease, the tenant will obtain his own repairs when something goes wrong and just send the owner the bill. A good tenant in a single-family house will usually handle such chores as snow shoveling, leaf raking, lawn mowing, and all other upkeep items that a multiunit resident will expect the owner to arrange or handle personally.

Next in order of risk are the various sizes of multiunit properties, with the two-flat ranking as the safest, but also the least profitable. However, the two-flat should not be overlooked for the first-time investor, says Richard Falstein, who specializes in rehabbing these properties. He notes:

> There are four good reasons to like two-flats. First, they can be picked up for $5000 to $6000 down. Second, they are appreciated by tenants because they provide semiprivacy, with a lawn and garage. Third, they're very readily salable after they're rehabbed, with many more potential buyers than a large building. One good market for them is young couples who can live rent-free on one level while developing equity. Fourth, there's no need for a union janitor. We usually handle yard maintenance by entering a maintenance contract with one of the tenants. And the tenant usually has more pride in the building than a paid janitor.

Most investors advise that you buy as many units as you have time and money to commit, though not more than six on the first-ever rehab effort. They point out that with as few as two units, if one of them is vacant, half your income is cut off, and mortgage payments cannot be met by the rents. With four units or six, even two vacancies can be tolerated for a while because the other tenants will meet the mortgage payments or come close. In that sense, they say the *more* units you have, the less the risk.

The last question you, the investor, have to answer concerning what you should buy is what can you afford? In the chapter on financing a rehab project, you will learn that it is possible to buy a building for less than 20 percent down in some circumstances, but do not count on that. The best building to rehab may not be the best on which to obtain financing. Thus, you may like a building specifically because it needs so much work that it is unusually cheap. However, the lender may turn it down for the same reason.

Furthermore, lenders who would loan you 80 percent of the value of a building that did not need any work might offer only a 70 percent loan if they have any extra qualms about you or the property. And, they are especially likely to ask for 30 percent down if you do not intend to live in a unit on the premises. So, having *some* cash or access to additional financing would be considered essential to buying a building to rehab.

Fortunately, many people who own a home have such reserves and do not even realize it. The appreciation in value of the typical house has been so great over the last 5 years that it may be worth a third to a half again what was paid for it. That means there is accumulated capital that is not being used, but can be easily tapped to make another real estate investment. It is not even necessary to sell the house to get that money out of it.

The trick is to refinance. That is, you take out a new mortgage at 80 percent of the current value of the home, pay off the old mortgage, and use the difference to finance your rehab project. As an illustration, if a house was purchased for $35,000 5 years ago, it might sell for $50,000 now because of inflation and rising demand. Refinancing would produce at least 80 percent of the $15,000 appreciation, or $12,000.

Lenders are happy to oblige when someone wants to write a new mortgage, because the current interest rate is likely to be higher than it was several years ago. Moreover, they are dealing with an established customer who they know makes the mortgage payments.

An interesting variation on refinancing if you need more than just the appreciated value of the house—that is, if you could use your original down-payment too—is to sell your home to an investor and lease it back. Such a practice is common on commercial real estate, but is just beginning to be utilized on residential property.

WHAT SHOULD YOU BUY? 7

The reason for this interest is that many investors are in the market looking for houses they can buy and rent to someone else. They would jump at the opportunity to sign a 5-year lease for rental of the home, especially with the current occupant. While you might have to accept escalation clauses so that rents rise every year, you would be relieved of the burden of rising property taxes that might equal the rent increases.

The way this plan works is that you simply sell the property to a home investor. Brokers know of these people and can direct you to them. You sign a 5-year lease (or whatever term is agreed upon), and take all of your money—downpayment, equity accumulation, and appreciation—out to use at your discretion.

The one drawback is that you would have to pay capital gains taxes on your profit. If you were buying another residential property that you intended to occupy and it were at least as expensive as the property you sold, this tax would be avoided. Since you do not plan to move from the house you have sold, that tax relief would not apply.

Still, the capital gains tax may not be such a burden because it is the most-favored treatment of profit from a sale. It is worth checking out with an accountant.

Other sources of help with financing—loans from parents, second mortgage, contract purchases, and other devices to raise the downpayment—will be discussed in the chapter on financing. Asking the seller to hold the mortgage also might be feasible, as will be seen in the same chapter.

The question remains as to how much debt to take on. The lender will probably have more to do with setting that boundary than you will. The lender will take a look at your family income, including husband and wife if both are employed, and decide how much you can afford. In a conventional house purchase, the limit is usually set at about two-and-a-half times gross income. If the family income is $30,000, then the lender would permit a purchase of $75,000.

Sometimes, a lender will stretch that limit for a family that seems almost certain to enjoy a rising income over the period of the mortgage. Moreover, on an income-producing property, the lender should take into account that you will have help meeting the mortgage payments from tenants in the building.

Therefore, if the neighborhood does not seem too risky and your plan for rehabbing the property seems realistic, the two-and-a-half times income formula might be stretched a bit.

At some point early in your quest for property, you should visit the mortgage officer of the most likely source for your loan. Tell that officer what you plan to do, explain your financial circumstances, and try to get a feeling or indication of what limits the institution might put on the size loan in which it would participate.

It is difficult to predict what each lender will do. If they know you from holding the loan on your home, they will be more inclined to go to extra lengths to help. If you are a stranger who seems to have a dreamer's scheme about how to get rich in a hurry, you will find the lender hard to persuade to back you.

Always play it conservatively with lenders. Give them to understand in the first interview that you are using great caution in your choice of property, obtaining expert counsel, and preparing to come in with a sound plan for the rehabilitation.

At the end of all of this analysis of what you should buy, the possibilities should be rather well-defined. You will know whether you want to buy a property where you intend to reside, what commitment you are able to make in terms of your own time, how much risk you are willing to take, and how much money you have to buy the building and improve it.

That is enough information to start the search, and eventually to choose the property, which is the subject of the next chapter.

2 | CHOOSING THE PROPERTY

SELECTING THE NEIGHBORHOOD

In the 100 years from 1872 to 1972, the red brick Victorian building near De Paul University in Chicago had five owners and appreciated in value from the original $2400 that it cost to build to the $22,000 it brought in October of 1972.

Then, dramatic changes started to occur in the area. Investors moved in and began rehabbing adjoining properties. Demand skyrocketed. In 1975, the building sold for $90,000.

The property enjoyed occasional minor refurbishment over the years, but not enough to account for so great a jump in value as occurred in the 3-year period from 1972 to 1975. The building just illustrates how important the choice of location can be and how profitable it can be to spot the uptrend early enough.

Not too early. One rehabilitated building cannot reverse a trend toward decay.

"Look for a block in which at least a third of the properties show some signs of renovation or improvement," says Richard Kaplan, an investor in several rehab projects in the Midwest. "Unless you are completely familiar with an area, I don't advise you to go in first."

The selected area must experience a change from a relatively low- to a higher-rent status, says Anthony Downs of the Brookings Institution, former head of Real Estate Research Corp. To make sound judgments about areas that might undergo such a change, Downs makes these recommendations:

- Avoid neighborhoods that are considered undesirable because of adverse social conditions, such as **high crime rate or dominance of very low-income families.**

- Seek areas in which rents are low because the properties are older and run-down, rather than where the neighborhood is considered undesirable.
- Look for areas located near potential anchors, such as parks, water (a lake, river, or ocean), downtown, or universities.
- Owner-occupants should dominate the area, rather than absentee landlords.
- The presence of a neighborhood organization that promotes community interests is a positive sign.
- Where local government is committed to neighborhood revitalization, the risk is reduced.
- Absence of any major problems of personal security is highly important.

Experienced rehab investors believe the matter of whether a neighborhood is receiving adequate services from the local government—especially police protection—to be crucial. Local governments sometimes abandon areas where street cleaners, trash collectors, and other employees are afraid to venture. Such neighborhoods are no place to invest.

The attitude of lenders toward a neighborhood is equally important. If mortgages are difficult to obtain in certain areas, other investors who might want to come in might be discouraged. On the other hand, if a few rehab projects already are underway in an area, you can be sure mortgage money can be found somewhere.

Some of the indications that a neighborhood might or might not be a good place to look for a building are highly visible. For example, for-sale signs can be a bad indicator if they exceed 5 percent of the properties in an area. On the other hand, *in combination with building permit signs,* they probably mean the owners are taking the occasion of rising property values to unload at a better price than they ever expected to get. Building permits are required to be displayed in every property where internal work of any consequence is occurring. A large number of building permits in an area is a sure sign that it is on the upgrade.

So is the presence of new commercial activity near the neighborhood unless the commercial areas are expanding into the residential. Then, an investor should call the local planning commission to find out what is happening. The area may be about to go entirely commercial, and, under those circumstances, it would be folly to spend money on a residential building. However, so long as confined in the commercial zone, the improvement of property by area merchants would indicate their continued confidence in surrounding residential neighborhoods.

Figure 2-1 Evidence of rehab work already going on in a neighborhood should encourage the investor considering property there.

Neat, well-maintained yards indicate that residents take pride in their properties and usually that the properties are largely owner-occupied.

New houses or apartment buildings being constructed within or near a neighborhood usually help boost confidence in the area because they indicate that the smart money still thinks there is a future there.

The class of people you see on the streets, especially at night, often tells a lot about the character of an area. A night visit is a good idea anyway, to see if it looks safe and has enough lighting. The people who work during the day are home then, and you can observe them on streets and see what kind of cars they drive.

These are the visual impressions (Figure 2-2). You can also get good verbal impressions by dropping in the local laundromat or buying an item in the drug store in order to engage local residents in conversations.

Ask about any unusual problems the neighborhood might have, such as flooding or water shortages or noisy air traffic. Merchants should be voluble about any problems they have with vandalism, theft, and personal injury. Ask if the police patrol often enough, whether they ever catch any criminals, and if they get convictions.

Surprisingly, some rehabbers do not consider the matter of good schools in a neighborhood to be of much importance. First of all, they do not particu-

12 | REHABBING FOR PROFIT

Figure 2-2 This thorn between two roses represents an opportunity for the investor because its run-down condition has not been corrected, though the two adjoining buildings have been rehabbed already.

larly want families with children in their apartments. Second, they are not likely to get them anyway. The apartment market in revitalized neighborhoods tends to consist of singles and young marrieds without children. When they eventually do add a family, they move into a house, usually in a suburban environment.

Therefore, investors would much prefer to see restaurants, shopping facilities, and entertainment nearby, because that is what their best potential market would most desire.

Learn how the people who live in the area get to work. Good public transportation may be a critical factor unless most residents go to work by auto. Then, it is important that the buildings have access to enough parking, preferably enclosed garages in cold climates.

If the emphasis in transportation is on commuting by train or bus, be certain that no reduction or closing down of the service is likely. The threat or reality of diminished service in the principal means of transportation to an area may be the main reason why it has fallen into decline.

After considering these factors, an investor should be able to identify a few areas or neighborhoods in which it seems wisest to concentrate. Then, as a last step, go see the local government. Talk to someone in the planning office who knows these areas. Find out if changes in the plans for the neighborhoods have been considered. Is there going to be more commercial activity there? What changes in zoning have recently occurred (you may be referred to the zoning commission)? Are any new highways or other government improvements anticipated? Have any projections been made as to the growth or future course of these areas? It is the job of planning and zoning people to give information to taxpayers to the extent that they know it. Do not be afraid to ask.

In fact, there are good sources all around to help you find out what you need to know about areas in which you may wish to invest. Some of them are listed on page 14.

INSPECTING THE BUILDINGS

After settling on a few areas that seem to offer favorable characteristics for a rehab investment, the next step is to narrow the search down to a few buildings that might be worth considering.

That search starts in one of two places: in newspaper advertisements for real estate or a real estate broker's office. Newspaper ads have become the marketplace for real estate buyers and sellers to meet. Some of the ads are placed by brokers; some, by owners trying to avoid a broker's commission. The latter often present interesting opportunities because owners sometimes are willing to bend more on price when they know they are saving the 6 or 7 percent commission that would be paid a broker.

More often, brokers place the ads. Note which ones offer properties in the neighborhoods you have chosen to concentrate on. Go visit them. Ask if they handle the type of property you are interested in. If so, have they sold any like it recently? What trends do they see in that neighborhood?

After a lot of probing, an investor can get a good fix on the broker. Then, go see another broker in the area. Compare what the second broker tells you with what the first said was happening. Maybe you can use both of them and perhaps a third or fourth who works that territory.

Remember that it does not cost the prospective buyer anything to use the services of a broker. The seller pays the commission. But, brokers must have prospective buyers or they are out of business. So the broker who believes you are sincere about wanting to purchase property can be an invaluable aid.

The most invaluable help the broker offers is listing cards (see Figure 2-3). Much information is contained on these cards—room sizes, special features, taxes, equipment and appliances that go with the property, comments on the condition of the property, and the asking price. There is also a picture of the building.

The broker arranges all these cards in sequence from the lowest- to the

REHABBING FOR PROFIT

Checkpoint	Source
How much rehabilitation already is occurring in the area?	Walking inspection to spot building permits. Municipal building department to examine permits in the area.
Are property values on the way up or down in the area?	Real estate brokers. City hall records of resales of particular properties, as indicated by tax stamps.
Is property being maintained?	Walking inspection of the area.
Are owners remaining in the area, or moving away and renting their property?	Area merchants. Real estate brokers.
Are commercial influences beginning to take over some residential property?	Municipal planning or zoning commission. Residents of the area.
Are municipal services adequate for the residents?	Area residents and merchants.
How good is the transportation?	Self-inspection and evaluation. Transit authority schedules and information.
Are there any plans to reduce or discontinue transportation lines to the area?	Community newspapers (ask the editor). Area residents. Municipal transit authority.
Has anything new been built in, or planned for, the area that may influence it?	Municipal planning commission. Community newspaper. Area merchants.
What do lending institutions think of the area?	Mortgage loan officers at the institutions. (If they are investing in the area, ask in what kinds of properties.)
What adult amenities are present?	Walking inspection. Community association. Ads in community newspaper.
Are there any nuisances?	Area residents and merchants.
What is the ratio of furnished to unfurnished apartments?	Inspection of posted for-rent signs on area buildings. Real estate brokers. Area residents.
What do properties in the area rent for?	Inspection of for-rent signs in the area. Real estate brokers.
How high is vacancy in rental buildings?	Mailboxes. (How many do not show names?)

CHOOSING THE PROPERTY | 15

FEATURE LIST

CONSTRUCTION & STYLE	CONSTRUCTION & STYLE
[X] A) BRICK	[ ] H) ROW HOUSE
[ ] B) BRICK/CONTEMPORARY	[ ] I) STUCCO
[ ] C) BROWN STONE	[ ] J) TOWNHOUSE
[ ] D) CONCRETE	[ ] K) VICTORIAN
[ ] E) FRAME	[X] L) VINTAGE
[ ] F) NEW CONSTRUCTION	[ ] M) OTHER
[ ] G) REHAB	

TYPE SHEET

Add: 861 WEST LAKESIDE City: CHGO L#:
Const & Style: BRICK - 1920'S   Area # 40
Apts: 7   Bsmt: FULL   Lot Size: 50 x 125   Elec: [X]220 [ ]110   Age: 1920'S   N 4650 W 861

Monthly Income:
1. 2,200 SQ. FT. PER FLOOR. 4+ BEDROOMS AND 2 BATHS

EXPENSES:
- Tax $
- Fuel $ PLEASE CALL
- Elec $
- Wtr $ LISTER FOR
- Ins $
- Misc $ ADDITIONAL
- $ INFORMATION
- Total $

Bath: CERAMIC Kit: PLASTER Gar: 3-CAR [3] Range
Walls: Walls: PLASTER Heat: STEAM [ ] Refr
Terms: OWNER MAY HOLD SECOND MORTGAGE [ ] A/C

Remarks: CURRENTLY 7 APARTMENTS. 1-4+ BEDROOM, 2-1 BEDROOM AND 2 BASEMENT APARTMENTS. HUGE ROOMS WITH 10' CEILINGS, OAK FLOORS, STAINED GLASS, LARGED COVERED PORCHES OFF LIVING ROOMS, BAY WINDOWS IN DINING ROOMS WITH FRENCH DOORS, EAT-IN KITCHENS. TO ENLARGE UNITS TO ORIGINAL FLOOR PLAN, REMOVAL OF HALLWAY WALL IS ONLY CONSTRUCTION NECESSARY.

GOOD TENANTS. OWNER MAY HOLD JUNIOR MORTGAGE TO QUALIFIED BUYER.

POSSIBLE TO BUY WITH 10-15% DOWNPAYMENT.

CONDEX 2-4 Units

Price: $265,000

Off: HOWARD ECKER RESIDENTIAL Ph: 280-1090
Slsp: LYNN FISCELLI

Figure 2–3 The broker's listing card provides vital information about property that is for sale.

highest-priced property. That makes it convenient to find the buildings in the investor's price range.

Some rehab pros look at hundreds of listing cards over a period of time, but actually go out to inspect only a few. Others look at almost everything in their price range, feeling that they might hit on a nugget that the rest of the market overlooked. It pays to check your brokers every few weeks and see what is new in the market or to have them contact you when something promising comes along. They will gladly do so if they take you to be a serious prospect.

A broker may try, however, to turn you over to a salesperson, rather than handling your search for property directly. That is acceptable, in some cases, but not if the salesperson is newly licensed and learning the job on your time or has no knowledge of the type property you are seeking.

You are the one who needs the experience gained by looking at many properties, not your brokers' employees. It is important to your making the right decision to see a number of buildings, so your comparisons will be valid.

The investor should think in terms of making two inspections of properties that look promising. The first, made by the investor personally, is the layman's evaluation. The second, only undertaken if the first impression is largely positive, would be made together with an expert on construction and costs, and the investor would have to pay for that expertise.

To start with, the investor can perhaps eliminate some properties simply by looking at them carefully from the exterior. Here are some things to evaluate:

- What is the condition of the grounds? Though some landscaping problems can be handled inexpensively and with dramatic results in the exterior appearance of a building, a lawn that must be replaced or trees that are dying or dead would be a different matter. A sunken area in the lawn could mean a broken storm or sanitary sewer.
- Does the house have any lean to it? If so, the structural foundation is unstable, and you should give it a pass. If there is no lean or tilt, even if it is an old building, it is probably still structurally sound.
- Do the foundation walls have any cracks? Cracks of ¼ inch or more need expert evaluation as to whether they represent an insoluble problem.
- Are the paved areas (driveways and patios) in good enough condition that they would not have to be repaved at a cost of $1 or more per square foot?
- Are gutters and downspouts rusted or sagging so much that they would have to be replaced?
- What is the condition of the windows and doors? Weather stripping and storm doors and windows are big pluses, if the building has them. Warping, rotting, and cracking signs in the areas around windows and doors could require expenditures to correct the problems. Be sure to point out these conditions, if they exist, to your expert and ask what it will cost to make proper repairs.
- Is the roof in good shape? The best most investors can do to examine the roof is to look at it through binoculars and try to spot missing shingles or obviously worn areas. It is well, though, when you meet the owner, to ask for the receipt from the last time the roof was replaced. Such records are kept for income tax purposes, so if the owner is reluctant to produce it, the roof is suspect. However, a roof lasts for 15 or 20 years, so your expert may find that it is okay.
- How about the chimney? While making a binocular inspection of

the roof, look at the chimney to see if there are missing bricks. They may indicate that the whole chimney will have to be replaced.
- If the property operates off a septic tank, how is the tank working? Soggy ground or odors around the septic tank mean you may have problems up to and including replacing the tank immediately.

Consider the exterior inspection to be the first test of whether even to go inside the building (Figure 2–4). But, remember that, if you find some of these items to be deficient, the property should not be automatically disqualified. After all, you are buying property to rehab it, and *something* is going to be wrong with it.

However, if too many problems are detected just by looking at the exterior, the conditions generally signal that the interior is just as badly in disrepair. Also, this first inspection helps you judge how much would have to be spent merely to cure the problems outside the building. That expense may already exceed what you are prepared to spend on the entire rehab job.

If no insurmountable or exceptionally expensive problems can be detected

Figure 2–4 Exterior inspection reveals many defects, but the important concern of the rehab investor is whether the defects can be cured within the economic realities of the property. *(Courtesy of Jerry Field.)*

on a lay inspection of the building exterior, the next step is to arrange an appointment to see the interior. That process may be more complicated than it seems. Most buildings are still occupied by tenants. In a several-unit building, that means making arrangements with all of the tenants, which may not be possible to accomplish so that every unit can be seen on the same visit.

It should be the broker's responsibility, not yours, to make these arrangements. The broker will confer with the owner of the building, who will set up the appointment.

Ask the broker to go with you, or have someone from the broker's office do so. Some tenants do not like the idea of having anyone in their apartments—especially anyone who is likely to ask them to vacate so the building can be rehabilitated. They also may have something against the owner that they would take out on you. So, go with someone who will take the heat if there is any to take.

If most of the apartments *do* turn out to be vacant, then you know you have a different problem. Tenants may have found the building unhabitable for some good reason. Of course, the explanation may also be that the owner let them know that the building would be sold and vacated, so they left early.

As you make the inspection, remember that you are looking for problem areas that can be cured so that they add value to the building. For example,

Figure 2–4 continued.

replacing a broken windowpane is just an expense. It adds no value at resale because any buyer would expect unbroken window panes. Therefore, you should insist that the seller bear that expense before you take over the property. On the other hand, cracked and peeling woodwork around a window penalizes the value of the house now, but can be cured easily so that it will add value when you resell the property.

On your inspection tour, take a pad or possibly a small recording device and note everything you observe that needs to be done. Later you can decide which items you will ask the seller to take care of and then get the others costed out. Do not try to deal with these matters during the inspection; just list them all.

The amateur inspector rarely has enough know-how to go beyond the cosmetic layer of a building. It is best left to an expert to get into the problems of the electric, cooling, heating, and plumbing systems—especially as to compliance with the local building codes.

The purpose of your inspection is to seek deficiencies that are more easily recognized and see whether it is even worthwhile to pay for an expert to look into the mechanical systems. Here are some deficiencies you can seek out on your own:

Insulation has become a doubly important factor in a building. It contributes to comfort by reducing drafts and cold areas, as always. Now, with energy costs soaring, it also saves money for the property owner. If a building does not have adequate insulation, you may have to provide it.

Look for insulation in the attic, where it should be at least 6, and preferably 8, inches thick; in the basement, where it should be in the ceiling if the basement is unheated; and around the windows and doors, where it is visible as weather stripping or storm windows and doors. Ask about wall insulation. It is doubtful that a rehab property will have it.

It is a fine thing and a definite plus if the insulation is reasonably adequate. It will save you heating and cooling costs every month that you own the property.

Individual metering for each unit means that tenants pay for their own energy costs—a great advantage to the owner. Without individual metering, the owner gets a single utility bill for all the apartments and must reflect the cost in the rents. Tenants have no incentive to hold those costs down, so they are higher than they should be.

Moreover, it is hard to catch up with a big jump in utility bills because they cannot be recaptured until the next rent increases. By then, energy costs may have soared again. If individual meters are absent, ask your expert, if you get that far, to estimate how much it would cost to put them in. Probably too much, but, if other electric work is extensive, it may be feasible.

A *dry basement* relieves the investor of one of the most expensive deficiencies to correct. The signs of water infiltration are rather easily detected, especially in a unit occupied by a tenant who makes no effort to conceal them. The owner may try to hide evidence of water in a basement by a new paint job on the floor or floorboards, but that too is a telltale sign.

Plumbing can be subjected to some tests, even by the layman. For example, run the faucets to see how the hot and cold water respond and if the flow is steady or irregular. Flush the toilet while the water is running to see if they affect each other. If one slows to a trickle, either the pipes are rusting or the water pressure is low in the area.

Especially important to test are any showers in the building. Few things anger a tenant more than a shower that runs alternately hot and cold after adjustment. It can be a difficult and expensive problem to correct.

Soundproofing is highly important in an apartment building where an investor expects to get the top rent dollar that a rehabbed unit can command. If adjoining apartments are occupied, see if you can hear anything from the next one. If the building is vacant, bring along a radio and play it loudly in one apartment while trying to hear it in the other.

There is not much that can be done inexpensively to improve soundproofing if the problem is severe. So, know how much of a problem you have before going into a rehab project, or you may not be able to keep tenants, and tenant turnover is deadly to profits.

Floors should be studied from two aspects. If they are uneven, that could mean an uneven settling of the foundation and structural problems. If they are in such bad shape that they would have to be replaced or carpeted over, the expense will be considerable.

However, floors that just need sanding or could be restored with a new stain job represent a curable deficiency that should pay for itself and more at resale time.

Window openings that have rotten areas or loose windows represent a rather serious problem. Remember that the windows are a primary source of heat escape. If they do not function well, they are more than just a nuisance; they are a financial drain.

Open and close each window to see what kind of problem you have and what will be necessary to cure it. If some are stuck or rattle back and forth because they are loose, try to get the seller to bear the expense of fixing them before the deal is closed. Repairing these problems yourself is not a recoverable cost (Figure 2–5).

Kitchens and bathrooms represent more value per square inch than any other rooms in the building. They are also most likely to be problem areas requiring expensive rehabilitation.

The first thing to learn about the *kitchen* is whether all the appliances are

Figure 2-5 Windows that are boarded up should be replaced by the seller, or their replacement cost deducted from the price of the sale. It will not repay the investor in added value on resale to make so ordinary a correction as window replacement.

included in the sale. Sometimes, the refrigerators or other appliances go with the seller, and they have to be replaced immediately in order to rent the apartments. Of those that remain, try to figure out which ones will survive your ownership of the property. Those that will not should be replaced as soon as possible, so they will help initial rent-up and can be amortized over a longer period of time (Figure 2-6).

Counter tops cost about $12 to $15 a foot to replace, so note any that will not be acceptable to more discriminating tenants. An unpleasant looking sink, with stains, chips, and scratches, also may need replacement.

Cabinet space may have to be increased for the rents you expect to receive. Some tenants consider the absence of enough cabinet space to be sufficient reason not to take an apartment or house. If there are enough cabinets, but they need reconditioning, you have no problem. That is a job the average investor can do or hire someone to do, and it is a recoverable cost at resale.

A leaky faucet or leaks below the sink should be repaired by the seller, because it is not a recoverable expense.

In the *bathroom,* the presence of a lot of tile can lead to heavy expense if the tile is worn or water has seeped behind it, and it must be replaced (Figure 2–7). If you can get away with a few replacement tiles, the problem is minimal.

Exhaust fans should be in working order. If they are not, it should be the seller's expense to repair them before closing. Check each one, in the kitchen and bathroom, to see if they are workable.

Room air conditioners usually can be purchased from the seller or tenants at a fraction of their original cost. If they are in good working order, it may be a good investment to buy those on the premises. An apartment will bring a better price if at least the bedrooms are air-conditioned. Paying an extra $120 for a room air conditioner might produce $10 a month in extra rent, and thus the cost would be amortized in a year. On your inspection, turn them on and see that they are functioning properly.

By considering the foregoing items, the investor can at least narrow the search down to one or two properties that a construction expert could look at for the additional information needed to make a more informed go or no-go decision.

At this point, you should have a list for each building that interests you of those items that require rehab work in order to get the rents you need to realize investment objectives. Divide this list into two parts, one part being comprised of those items that will eventually add value to the building and the other, those

Figure 2–6 Besides replacing or adding appliances to this kitchen, additional cabinet space may be needed and probably additional electrical wiring.

Figure 2-7 An extreme example of a bathroom in which appliances and tiles probably will have to be replaced.

that simply must be done so the property will be in acceptable condition to be rented. The latter items are those you want to try to get the seller to handle in advance of closing.

Ideally, you should get more than a dollar back in rents and potential resale profit from each dollar invested in the rehabilitation effort. You certainly *would not* get your money back from repairing windows and doors that stick, light switches that do not work, a shower nozzle that drizzles instead of flows, or locks that are broken. Or from repairing or replacing a leaky roof, for that matter.

However, your tenants will expect these repairs to be made when they occupy the property and will call them quickly to your attention if they are not. The seller of even a run-down building usually can be talked into doing these repairs—or at least some of them—if you negotiate the matter forcefully.

Your second list of what needs to be done that will increase value and impress tenants enough that they will happily pay the rent should be the more important one. Try to figure out what materials will be required to accomplish these improvements—how much paint, how many days to rent a floor sander, how much carpet to replace, how much wallpaper, and all the other materials that will be needed.

Visit a good hardware store and get prices on all the materials needed. If you do not know how much paint it would take to cover 9×12 foot room, the hardware merchant will. For carpet estimates, take approximate measurements to a carpet store and see what is available at different prices.

When other people are going to do the work for you, labor costs must be figured as well. They can range from the $2 an hour that you would pay a young relative or acquaintance to scrape or paint to the $15 an hour that you would pay a skilled carpenter or plumber.

In the end, you should have a reasonable estimate of the material and labor costs for rehabbing those flaws you found in the property—before your consultant has seen it. This information will tell you how close you would be to your budget for the rehab job, exclusive of work that might be required on the mechanical systems.

GETTING EXPERT ASSISTANCE

At some point in the process of searching for the right property to buy, the investor exhausts his own knowledge and must ask someone more expert about construction to make the deeper inspection that will reveal the *true extent* of the rehab work that will be required.

Where do you find such people? Start with the broker and lender. Ask them for the names of people who are especially knowledgeable about rehab. Some professionals are used to dealing with *new* materials and modern structures. They do not know how to inspect an older property with the authority you need. Others specialize in rehab, and they are well known to brokers and lenders, who have dealt with them before.

When you are ready to select such a person, you will be faced with the choice of an architect, a contractor, a representative of one of the home inspection services, or a real estate appraiser. Depending on the circumstances, one of these professionals probably will suit your needs better than the others.

For example, if the rehab job involves a house that the investor intends to occupy, then an architect might be the best choice. You can tell the architect what you want to do with the property, and the architect can tell you if it is feasible. Later, you might want to use the architect's services to develop plans for the whole rehab job. This professional would be much more qualified than any of the others to suggest materials, imaginative floor plans, special lighting, room additions, and other ideas that would produce a real knockout rehab job. In addition, the architect would have sufficient knowledge of the mechanical systems to spot deficiencies, though perhaps not to estimate the cost of curing them.

An architect would charge some reasonable fee, probably $100 to go over a house for you, possibly another $50 a unit to look at a multiunit building.

A contractor might be the person you turn to for most of the work if you go ahead with the rehab project. The contractor's skills lie in handling the construction; not in suggesting what should be done, which is the architect's forte. A contractor, bidding for rehab jobs almost every day, usually has an easy handle on costs. The contractor is able not only to tell you what is wrong in the mechanical systems, but how to take care of it and what the cost might be.

A contractor who considers you to be a good prospect for further business will be likely to keep the inspection fee at a minimum, perhaps $100 for a multiunit building of modest size. Otherwise the fee could be as high as $200 to size up a several-unit property.

Private inspection services have become established in most major cities and can be found under the classified telephone book category "Building Inspection Services." They will charge about $100 for a single unit and as much as $50 per additional unit. Some will give you a warranty that what they found was an accurate picture of the deficiencies of the property and nothing of importance was missed. But, the warranty is of little real value because it only means you get your inspection fee returned if a serious problem is not identified. Still, a qualified building inspector does this work for a living, and knows how to dig into a house to see what the problems are. Many inspectors have engineering training.

Building inspectors from a private service may be the best answer if you do not think you will be needing an architect or want to get committed to dealing with a contractor yet. However, a private building inspector cannot be expected to give you reliable cost figures about what it would take to cure the defects that are found. You will get a guess, if you ask, but it is just a guess.

The real estate appraiser tells a client something the other professionals do not—an opinion of how much the property is actually worth. If that information is important to you, the appraiser may be a better choice than the architect, contractor, or building inspector.

It should be noted that appraisers are not especially trained in construction. All they want to do when inspecting a home is to establish that it is in acceptable enough condition that it compares to other buildings in the market. An appraiser will estimate what the remaining lives of various components, such as the heating system, are likely to be, but will not take the hard look that you need at plumbing and wiring. (The services performed by an appraiser will be discussed further in the chapter on financing a rehab project.)

Because of the costs involved in using these experts, the investor wants to use them sparingly and select the right one for the purpose. The kind of information you should request when employing such a consultant would include:

In what condition is the heating plant? A furnace that is more than 20 years old should be suspect, unless it has been kept in first-rate condition—unlikely in a building that is otherwise run-down. One of the major expenses you can run into is replacement of a furnace, so be sure it is working and working efficiently. Otherwise, heating costs are going to be exorbitant and a severe drain on the investment.

Does the hot-water heater have sufficient capacity? Remember that your new tenants are going to be more demanding than those previously living in the building because they will be paying far greater rents. If the hot water runs out frequently, they will be hard to retain as tenants—not to mention all the complaints you are going to have to hear.

What would it cost to add air-conditioning for the building? Rents may be boosted by as much as 20 percent in some areas of the country if the units are air-conditioned. That means you might pay for the cost of air-conditioning the building within 2 or 3 years, especially if the building has warm-air heat rather than hot-water heat. It is 15 to 25 percent cheaper to add air-conditioning if the heating system is forced warm air.

How adequate is the electric system? One of the great problems with older buildings, even those constructed as recently as 20 years ago, is that the capacity to handle all of the appliances and equipment used in the home today has been greatly exceeded. Certainly, the kitchen may be deficient both in capacity and in available outlets.

When getting a consultant's advice on the electric system (as well as the plumbing system), be aware that the problem may be underestimated because it is difficult to tell how serious the matter is until you go "behind the walls."

Does the plumbing work adequately? The more durable types of plumbing materials, such as plastic, brass, and copper pipes, came along after most buildings in this country were erected. The old iron pipes tend to rust inside, and the rust reduces water pressure below acceptable limits. They may have to be replaced at a plumber's cost of $10 to $14 an hour, plus materials.

In what shape are the roof and chimney? Maybe you do not want to climb up there and look at them, but your consultant should. Ask the consultant to examine any fireplaces in the building too, to be sure they are workable.

Next, the consultant should take a close look at the foundation. In an older home, some settling is expected. Differences in heights of adjacent sides for inside cracks would indicate problems.

Finally, you may want your expert to advise you concerning the possibility of changing the layout, perhaps combining two small rooms into one or opening an entry between two rooms to make the floor plan work better. That usually means removing or cutting into walls. Such schemes may have everything going for them except the structure of the building. Your ideas may involve taking out walls that help hold up the building or putting unacceptable weight on elements of the structure that are not capable of bearing it.

Even your ideas to finish an attic may be nixed by an adviser who finds that ceiling joists are not strong enough to support the new floor without additional shoring.

It is especially important to obtain from the expert an opinion as to violations of the building code that are observed and the cost to bring them into compliance. In general, you want to know the cost to cure everything that is deficient, but especially those items that would get you into trouble with the building inspector.

For most rehabilitation jobs—all but cosmetic, paint-up, clean-up type work—you will have to get a building permit from the municipal building commission. That usually amounts to an invitation for the building inspector to come out to look at the property.

However, an inspection by the local government representative is not all bad. The municipal employee will tell you exactly what needs to be done to meet the city building code, and that code is a document that is supposed to protect people from anything unsafe on the property.

At this point, the consultant will give you some kind of written report. It is important to have this report when you negotiate, because the flaws can be pointed out to the seller as a way to drive a better bargain. However, for the fee, you should not expect an elaborate report. Sometimes, it is just a form with space for comments where appropriate.

Try to get the expert to go a step further and give you, if not write down, an estimate of how much it will cost to cure those items that it is necessary to deal with in the rehab phase.

Now, you have two lists—the one you made on your own inspection and the consultant's. And, you should have some idea of the cost to do the job. Before deciding that you know everything that is feasible to learn about the physical property, go one step further. Pay a visit to the local government offices and look the property up in the assessor's records and the building inspector's office.

There is a veritable history of the property awaiting the curious citizen at the various offices of the municipal government. For example, at the tax assessor's office, you will find what the appraiser for the assessment authority last judged the value of the building to be. If you are interested in more than one building, you can compare the assessments and perhaps learn why the appraiser assigned one a higher value than the other.

The assessor probably will also have records of when the property was sold and how much it sold for, as indicated by the tax stamps that were purchased. Tax stamps can be somewhat misleading if the buyer went out of his way to confuse later purchasers by paying for more stamps than necessary. Such a strategy rarely is employed. In most cases, the $2 to $5 per $1000 that buyers typically purchase will tell you by simple multiplication how much was paid.

Another office, probably the building department, will even have details of the mortgage loans taken out on the property over the years and the lender's name. The latter could be helpful information as a lead to a lending institution that previously had been willing to finance the same property.

The building department or commission also will have a record of all building permits taken out to improve the property. Thus, you can check on the age of the furnace, the roof, the electric system, and any other changes made in the building that were of sufficient magnitude to require a building permit.

Finally, check with the zoning and planning commission as to any recent rezoning nearby, any easements that the property may have, and any other details about the property by someone other than the owner. The city might have a right to dig a slit trench through an area of your property where you wanted to build an addition.

Because each municipal government sets up its records in a different way, there is no general rule as to which department has which information. The place to start is the assessor's office in almost any local government. From there, you will be directed to where other information that you need is stored.

With all of the information collected on the *physical* aspects of the building, you are ready to consider whether it makes sense from the standpoint of the numbers. Will it be profitable, and at what price must it be purchased to produce that profit? These are questions to which the next chapter responds.

3 | HOW MUCH IS IT WORTH?

Even if the first building the investor sees appears to have all the characteristics of an ideal rehab opportunity, it is essential that a half dozen or more additional properties be evaluated before returning to the first. The educational value of seeing several buildings is important; the data to be gathered from such a survey is *critically* important.

Until the data on several income-producing properties have been analyzed, it is difficult to make an informed estimate of what income to expect, how much vacancy is typical for the area, and what comparable property sells for in the area.

On every income-producing building, the real estate broker or owner will supply a one-page "operating statement" that purports to tell the income the building brings in during a year and the expenses to operate that building. By collecting operating statements on several properties, the investor can accumulate reasonable, if not always believable, evidence as to the various benefits and costs of ownership of property in areas that seem to offer investment opportunity. Operating statements can be highly inaccurate unless they are accompanied by leases and rent records, as well as tax returns—preferably for several previous years.

Even then, errors in the estimates of income and expenses can occur, perhaps not even by design. Such errors must be discovered by the investor, for as will be seen, they affect the market value of the property by as much as six to ten times their worth. That is because investors tend to buy income-producing real estate on a basis of several times the net income after all expenses, vacancy, and bad debt are taken into account.

Therefore, each item of expense must be examined carefully, to see not only whether it is legitimate, but also whether it might not offer opportunity for reduction. For every dollar that you reduce expenses, you increase the return on the property and boost its market value by several times that dollar amount.

ESTIMATING RENTAL INCOME

Before dealing with expenses, you must find out how much rental income the property actually figures to bring, both now and after it is rehabilitated. That means the investor must make a rental market survey in the area in which a building that is under consideration (hereafter to be called the "subject building") is located.

That involves visiting as many buildings as possible on which a vacancy sign is posted. It is better in making this survey to pose as a prospective tenant. Most property owners do not appreciate showing their apartments to potential competitors. You also can see how tenants in that building are treated and how much information is given to them.

In looking at each rental unit in the neighborhood, compare it with those in the building in which you might invest. See if the rooms are as large and as well-maintained. Make these comparisons with the subject property not only as it stands, but also as it will be after it is rehabilitated. Now, make some subjective judgments, just as the market does, and try to answer these questions about every unit that is for rent in the neighborhood:

- Would I pay the rent asked for this unit?
- Is the property more or less attractive as a rental unit than those in the subject building? In terms of rent asked, how much more or less attractive is it?
- If the unit is occupied, what kind of people live there? Are they the type that I would want in my building? Why are they moving?
- Is the building as attractive from the outside?
- Is its location as good as the subject property?
- Is it the only unit available in the building, or does there seem to be a substantial amount of vacancy?

By making such judgments as these about as many rental units in the area as is feasible to inspect, an investor should be able to decide whether the rents shown by the owner of the subject building are in line with the market, as well as what rents could be obtained in other buildings just as good or better.

As a valid check against these subjective judgments, keep track of each unit that is for rent during your survey. Note how long it takes for it to be rented and whether the owner has to come down in price to obtain a tenant. Owners who must accept a vacancy or cannot rent an occupied apartment for several months probably have tried to obtain more rent than the building or the neighborhood warranted.

After a proper rental market survey, you will know the range of rents for units of the approximate size of those in the subject building. Then, you can

HOW MUCH IS IT WORTH? | 31

take a hard and perceptive look at the "rent schedule" that the owner shows on the operating statement of the building in which you might be interested.

Normally, the scheduled rents are high because they represent what the owner *thinks* each apartment would obtain in rental, rather than what it actually obtains. That may be due to the owner listing the rents at levels he *might* be able to get when current leases expire. (Then again, he might *not* be able to get those rents.)

The operating-statement rents also may reflect the owner's optimism that the property will never suffer a vacancy or any loss of rental because a tenant moves out or fails to pay the rent for some reason.

So the investor will need to make out realistic rent schedules for the building both as it stands and as if it were upgraded. Vacancy must also be considered, as well as some allowance for bad debt. The result of this analysis will be the development of one of the three important figures in deciding what to pay for a property, that is, the gross income or gross operating income.

In evaluating the rents each unit in a building might obtain, the investor cannot just lump them all together and decide the studios will bring X dollars and the one-bedroom units Y dollars, and so forth. Some units in a building may be more difficult to rent than others. Perhaps they are affected by street noise, or they may have little light or an ugly view. These units can throw off the estimate of potential income or create a higher vacancy factor than anticipated. The better units will produce more income, and the rent schedule for the property should reflect that fact.

Do not, then, in estimating the return from rents, equalize all units of each size without considering their desirability. In surveying other buildings, try to pick the most similar to each apartment in the subject property and decide whether the subject unit would rent for more or less if both were available to prospective tenants at the same time.

Some units in the subject building may include air conditioners, another factor that would create a higher rental value for one of two otherwise similar units.

In figuring gross income, the investor should not forget the real or potential income from the rental of garage space that may be part of the property. The building also may include vending machines, such as coin-operated washers and dryers. Or such equipment might be added to the building as another source of profit.

The goal of the investor should be to include all possible income from the building—rental and miscellaneous income—because that is the basis for refinement to an estimate of what the building is worth as it stands. In a separate column, list all the income that might be realized after the building is rehabilitated because that is the basis for determining if the investment eventually will produce a satisfactory return.

Next, the investor must try to estimate a likely percentage of vacancy and rent loss due to nonpayment by tenants. Ideally, this factor also should be measured in the market, that is, by how great the vacancy and rent loss have been in similar buildings. The experience of property owners in the same area with comparable property can be measured to some extent by noting signs and advertisements during the rental market survey. In an area where rehabbable property is likely to be found, the vacancy may be higher than for other neighborhoods for the good reason that the property is run-down.

National averages suggest that 4 to 6 percent is a normal loss in gross income from vacancy and rent loss. Certainly, that is a figure the investor should strive to achieve after a building has been upgraded.

It can be good news, not bad news, if the subject building is running a higher vacancy than the neighborhood as a whole. That means better management and maintenance, plus physical improvements contemplated by the rehabilitation, would at least bring the vacancy factor up to the level of the rest of the neighborhood.

The investor should try to find out why vacancy has been high if the subject property shows a factor higher than similar property. Perhaps the present owner just has an unpleasant attitude toward tenants that drives them away. Or, the current owner may not provide services that a new owner would. Or, the building just may be so poorly maintained that few people would want to live there at any rent in its existing condition.

Turnover must be accepted as a fact of life in a rental building. Depending on the number of units and the type building, turnover should occur once every 2 or 3 years in every unit. Sometimes, those units cannot be rented immediately, so they will return no income for a month or more. Vacancy must be taken into account and deducted from the income in even the best managed buildings.

FINDING THE NET INCOME

With rents and other income fully taken into account and vacancy and bad-debt loss deducted, the investor will arrive at one of the key components needed to estimate the value of the property, namely the gross income. The second of these components is net income, the adjusted gross income minus all expenses that relate to the operation of the building.

In studying the potential expenses of a building, the investor should be trying to obtain some guidance as to not only how much these costs are likely to be, but also how much they could be reduced by intelligent and careful management. As will be seen, most costs of operating a building can be reduced in one way or another. Such reduction contributes to an owner's profit margins.

The seller's operating statement probably will not be set up in the ideal way concerning expenses, that is, not the way that is recommended by the Institute of Real Estate Management or the federal government. In most categories, the seller's estimates of expenses cannot be regarded as reliable anyway. They are more revealing in the percentages of expenses shown in each category, as compared to the percentages in other buildings in the area, than in the raw numbers.

For example, if maintenance expenses in one building greatly exceed the average for others, as measured by the percentage of total expenses, then a problem area may be easily detected. Perhaps most operating statements that you have collected show that maintenance expenses total about 10 percent of all expenses, but the subject building shows that category (or any of its elements) to be much higher than 10 percent. The investor should find out why. The same is true if one category is much lower for the subject building than for other investment property.

You can make some easy judgments about the ratios in comparable buildings by dividing the total expenses claimed for a building into each separate expense item shown on the operating statement. That will give you a percentage for each item that can be compared easily both to national and neighborhood averages on other operating statements.

The categories of expenses that professional property managers list are administrative, operating, maintenance, taxes and insurance, service, and other payroll. Consider them one at a time in estimating current and future expenses for a building.

Administrative Expenses

Administrative expenses include management, advertising, legal, auditing, architect's or engineer's fees, telephone and building-office expenses, and office supplies used by the owner.

These expenses often run 5 to 10 percent of all costs that a building owner incurs, and they are one of the best areas for the investor to realize savings. By handling all management yourself (how to do it will be explained in a later chapter), you may be nullifying most of an expense that a previous owner may have been paying.

However, not all of this expense category can be eliminated. It will probably be necessary to advertise apartments when there is a turnover. Legal fees may be incurred when it is necessary to try to collect a potential rent loss or take a tenant to court over a lease violation. An audit for tax purposes and perhaps a part-time bookkeeper to record and pay bills will add to this expense item. So will the cost of preparing and mailing rent notices.

Of course, if the investor does not have the time or inclination to deal with these matters—essentially consisting of paying the bills, keeping the books, advertising the apartments, and sending out rent notices—an expense item must be included for the fee paid someone else to handle them.

Operating Expenses

Operating expenses include everything that goes into keeping the building running on a day-to-day basis. Some items under this category include electricity, heating fuel, gas other than heating fuel, water and sewer, supplies, building services, and any miscellanous expenses that apply to operating the building. Consider these items one at a time:

The expense of electricity can be calculated rather closely by looking at the seller's tax form or asking for actual receipts. Owners do not usually play around with these figures because they can be checked rather easily.

Under electricity would come the power for tenant areas, unless they are metered separately so that the tenant pays them; electricity for public areas of the building (corridors and stairways, among others); air-conditioning, but not heat; exterior lighting; and everything else that shows up on the electric bill.

As energy costs have risen, so has the cost of electricity in some areas. However, power companies are regulated as to their rates, and the unit cost of electricity does not increase as rapidly, provided that the amount of power consumed does not rise.

In considering what electricity might cost after rehabilitation, remember that tenants paying higher rents probably will have more appliances that use electric power. They may be provided with air-conditioning or may obtain window units of their own, thus increasing electricity expenses for the owner.

A property owner is indeed fortunate if apartments in a building are individually metered so that the tenant absorbs the amount of energy consumed and any increases that may occur. For one thing, the tenant will be more careful if the cost of electricity comes out of his pocket, than if it is a landlord expense. The feasibility of adding individual meters rather than a single meter for the whole building will be discussed later in this book.

It is possible, but not likely in an older building, that electricity also heats the building. If so, it makes even more sense to try to pass that cost directly along to the tenant by individual metering.

Whether it is electricity, gas, oil, coal, or any fuel, a separate expense item should be established for heating fuel. And, heating fuel should be the only consideration in this item of expense—not gas used for cooking, air-conditioning, or hot water.

This item is one of the most difficult to anticipate, especially in cold climates where harsh winters and shortages have caused fuel costs to soar. Even if tenants pay their own heating costs, a building owner must heat the common areas of a building—hallways, stairs, laundry areas, and so forth.

However, this item also is one that an owner can work to hold to current levels or reduce. Better insulation, for instance, can result in great savings in heating costs. Utilities often will provide free inspections and advice as to how this expense item can be reduced or the heating plant made more efficient.

When an apartment uses gas for cooking, air-conditioning, hot water, and other purposes (but not heating fuel, which is considered separately), a separate expense item should be included. Usually, all gas-fueled items are covered by a single utility bill, so it is difficult to separate how much expense is represented by heating and how much by the other usages. The way to separate them is to take the lowest summer month, when heat probably was never used, and multiply that number by 12. Such an exercise provides a reasonable estimate of gas expenses other than heating.

Water costs usally are estimated accurately by the seller because they represent a rather minor item of expense. They might also include sewerage charges, or those costs might be billed separately. It is well to check this item with the utility if it appears to be out of line with estimates on other operating statements. If it is unusually high in the subject building, this expense item could indicate a wholly outdated plumbing system that would need replacement at great cost.

Water expenses can be reduced somewhat and may represent a curable area of waste. Leaky pipes or faucets, overuse of water in sprinkling the lawn, and other areas of loss may be eliminated or minimized for savings to the owner.

Supplies include all janitorial items, but not paint or other decorating materials (a maintenance item). This portion of the operating expenses should be minor, consisting mainly of cleaning materials, replacement light bulbs for the common areas, and other minor supplies. Little saving can be realized in this category.

In the area of miscellaneous building services, window washing, exterminating, and rubbish removal may represent some opportunities for savings if the investor is willing to take on some of these responsibilities. More likely, however, it will make sense to continue existing contracts or arrangements for these services. The seller should be willing to provide copies of any contracts that exist for these services and others that are included under the maintenance category.

Maintenance Expenses

Maintenance expenses offer the best potential for reducing expenses charged against income. Interior and exterior maintenance and repair, grounds maintenance, and painting and decorating all present opportunities for cost reductions from what a previous owner might have been willing to absorb. The fourth item in this major category, security, might add to your costs.

Under interior and exterior maintenance, property managers consider the routine costs of maintaining and repairing boilers, air conditioners, plumbing, and heating units to be accountable expenses. They also list maintenance of the building's television antenna, fire protection equipment such as fire extinguishers, small hand tools, tuck-pointing, and roof repair of a minor nature as part of this expense category.

Obviously, an investor can reduce these costs significantly by handling the work personally, instead of employing someone else to do it. Especially is this true for exterior painting and cleaning. In fact, cleaning can represent a substantial expense in buildings with lobbies or long corridors and stairways that are common to all units. Whereas, in many buildings, tenants handle much of the cleaning of areas near their units, the owner may at least provide a deep-cleaning once a year, for which there are labor and material costs in most cases.

After rehabilitation, a building should be kept clean and attractive or much of the effect of the upgrading can be lost. It is smart management to check regularly to see that the common areas are neat. That may mean employing someone to inspect those areas regularly and clean them up if they become unsightly.

Usually, a building will conform to the fire code in the equipment that is provided. However, it would be well to find out for sure and try to get the seller to agree that it is the seller's responsibility and expense to bring the building into fire-code compliance.

Minor repairs undoubtedly will be necessary when something breaks down. It is not possible to estimate how often these problems will occur or how much it will cost to make the repairs. The best source would seem to be the amount that the building has carried as an expense item in the past, with comparisons with other buildings of its type on which operating statements are available.

Snow removal can be a big item under grounds maintenance in many areas of the country. The landlord often must assume responsibility for clearing the walks and steps or at least providing salt for them. If this job does not interest the investor, find out how it has been done in the past. Perhaps a tenant can be persuaded to do the chore for a modest reduction in rent. Or maybe the next-door neighbor could be employed to handle your snow problem, as well as his own.

Caring for the lawn, feeding and watering shrubs and flowers, and generally maintaining the landscaping can be another big expense item. Again, find out how it was done in the past, and decide how much commitment you care to make to doing it yourself.

Ground maintenance supplies, such as fertilizer, hoses, sprinklers, and other equipment, should be included in this category. If the seller's supplies are in good condition, it might be a worthy investment to buy them.

Maintenance of outside lights also should be considered a part of the grounds maintenance item.

Another part of the major category of maintenance expenses is interior painting and decorating. This painting and decorating has nothing to do with the rehabilitation of the building. It covers expenses an owner will incur when a tenant moves and the apartment must be put in good order for the next tenant. Washing, painting, or papering of the walls and replacement of carpeting, draperies, furnishings, and light fixtures may be anticipated as well. Replacements should be listed and taken into account in a different item called "reserve for replacement" because they are considered capital rather than current expenditures and thus should not be counted as expenses in a single year, but over several years. The number of years will depend on their probable life.

An investor might hope to minimize this expense by handling most of the work and only paying for materials needed. However, if labor costs are likely, they should be included in this category.

Security could be the most troublesome category and the one most likely to cost more than an owner currently spends after a building has been rehabilitated. Even while it is being rehabbed, security may be a serious concern because valuable materials and tools may have to be left at the site.

A building in a bad area needs special protective devices—burglar alarms, heavy locks, window guards, and the like, which may not be necessary in better neighborhoods. Often, the seller has installed some of these devices, but perhaps not enough to keep the building as secure as tenants paying higher rents after rehabilitation would expect. Therefore, there may be an immediate expense both to protect tenants better and to secure materials and equipment being used in the rehabilitation.

The inevitable expenses, *taxes and insurance,* figure to be areas where it will be difficult for the investor to cut costs. In fact, they may well become larger expenses in a hurry.

The tax on a building probably will range from 12 to 18 percent of the gross income. If the seller has been paying less, do not figure that the low rate will continue. As the neighborhood improves or your building takes on an improved appearance, the assessor takes notice. Tax appraisals of the property figure to reflect the upgrading within 1 or 2 years after it occurs.

However, if the tax rate appears high—exceeding 18 percent of the gross income—the property may not be profitable because that is such a large bite. Perhaps that rate can be appealed, especially if it is out of line with the percentages of gross income common to other buildings in the area. (Again, review the operating statements you have collected as a check against the subject building.)

The methods for appealing a high property tax rate will be discussed in a later chapter. But, it is well to know at this point that the subject building either is in line with others of its type in an area or out of line—either high or low. A trip to the city or county assessor's office would be worth the effort. Learn how often properties are reappraised, when the last reassessment occurred, what the tax rate was last year, and what it will be this year and next. Sometimes, buildings are only reappraised by the assessor's office every fourth year. That usually means the taxes will be stable for that whole period.

On the other hand, if the fourth year for reappraisal is about to arrive, you can be sure that the tax will go up, perhaps significantly, especially if the neighborhood is improving.

The insurance expenses of the building almost certainly reflect less coverage than the 80 percent of value necessary to assure full replacement cost if the building is destroyed by fire or disaster. It definitely will not cover the building adequately after it is rehabilitated.

It is worthwhile to ask to see the insurance policy in force for other purposes than to see how much coverage is provided. If the seller says his policy covers the full 80 percent of value of the building (not the land), you can see how much he really thinks the building is worth. This information might be useful in negotiating the sale. You also will discover which insurer has been willing to provide coverage in the past and at what premium—worth knowing if the property later proves difficult or expensive to insure.

Remember to include all insurance costs in this category. That means fire, liability, theft, boiler explosion, and any worker's compensation involved if a janitor or other outside salaried worker is employed.

Service Expenses

Service expenses likely will represent a small part of an investor's costs. The principal subcategory here is recreational amenities, including the cost to operate and maintain swimming pools and game rooms. However, if the building has either of these facilities or just an area of the basement where pool, ping pong, and other games are available, the cost of supplies and replacement should be included here.

If laundry equipment is provided, some expenses may be incurred, even if the equipment is coin-operated washers and dryers. A service contract might be in force or needed to maintain this equipment.

Finally, there are *other payroll* expenses, including the fair-market rent of an apartment that the investor might provide to someone who handles maintenance and management of a building. The gross income should have shown the full rent likely to be obtained for each apartment, so this category should show any concessions in that rent for people who do chores in the building. Perhaps one apartment dweller receives $25 less than the going rate on rent because he handles all the minor repair problems of other tenants or keeps the hallways clean.

Whatever payments the seller has been making to tenants or outsiders should be analyzed to see if these expenses are necessary. The investor may want to take on these chores to reduce expenses.

After considering all of these factors, the investor should have a good idea just what it will cost to manage, maintain, and operate the subject building. As a reminder of the factors to be considered in each of the six main categories, here is a comprehensive checklist:

Administrative Expenses
- [ ] Accounting
- [ ] Advertising
- [ ] Auto expenses associated with the building
- [ ] Commissions (to rental agencies, ad agencies, etc.)
- [ ] Legal fees
- [ ] Licenses, permits
- [ ] Management
- [ ] Office supplies
- [ ] Telephone

Operating Expenses
- [ ] Air-conditioning
- [ ] Appliances and equipment
- [ ] Electricity
- [ ] Garbage removal
- [ ] Gas

- ☐ Heat
- ☐ Janitorial supplies
- ☐ Oil
- ☐ Sewer
- ☐ Trash removal
- ☐ Water

Maintenance Expenses
- ☐ Carpentry
- ☐ Cleaning
- ☐ Draperies
- ☐ Electric systems
- ☐ Elevator
- ☐ Exterior maintenance
- ☐ Exterminating
- ☐ Fire protection
- ☐ Fixtures
- ☐ Floor coverings
- ☐ Gardening
- ☐ Hardware
- ☐ Interior maintenance
- ☐ Landscaping
- ☐ Maintenance supplies
- ☐ Mechanical systems
- ☐ Painting and decorating
- ☐ Plumbing
- ☐ Security
- ☐ Television antenna
- ☐ Window washing

Tax and Insurance Expenses

INSURANCE
- ☐ Fire
- ☐ Liability
- ☐ Theft
- ☐ Boiler explosion
- ☐ Worker's compensation

TAXES
- ☐ Personal property
- ☐ Real estate

Service Expenses
- ☐ Recreational amenities
- ☐ Laundry facilities and supplies
- ☐ Parking

Other Payroll Expenses
☐ Janitorial
☐ Laborers
☐ Payroll fringes
☐ Payroll taxes

It is possible to get a general idea as to how much of your expense dollar will go for each of these categories by purchasing the annual Income/Expense Analysis of the Institute of Real Estate Management, available for $15 from the Institute at 430 North Michigan Avenue, Chicago, Illinois 60611. Though the publication contains a mass of data, including breakdowns by geographical area, it does not cover buildings smaller than twelve units, so the data are not directly applicable to most small investors.

But, to give the investor some idea as to how these expenses run in buildings that are low-rise and contain twelve to twenty-four units, here are percentage figures for a recent year (1977):

Administrative expenses	12.3 percent
Operating expenses	23.0 percent
Maintenance expenses	17.2 percent
Taxes and insurance	35.5 percent
Other payroll and services (combined)	11.9 percent

One additional item needs to be considered, even though it does not show on most operating statements prepared by sellers. Investors inevitably will be required to replace such items as stoves, refrigerators, and other appliances that are provided to tenants. They also will have to provide new furniture and accessories in lobbies, carpeting in hallways, and perhaps laundry equipment and other large items that wear out or grow outdated over a period of time.

To make these replacements, investors must hold back an amount called "reserve for replacement." Each month, an expense of ownership should be the withholding of an amount of money sufficient to make replacements as they are required.

This reserve may never be drawn upon. The building may be sold before it is needed. However, it can be held in an interest-bearing account, so the investor loses little by setting it aside and gains a valuable reserve if replacement is needed.

Some items that need early replacement probably will be accounted for in the rehabilitation. Those that are put off for the present should be listed and their probable replacement cost totaled. Then, working on a basis of how much additional life these items seem to have, a schedule can be developed to decide how much reserve is required.

Thus, if carpeting seems certain to need replacement within the next 3 years, and it will cost $1200 to replace, the reserve for replacement should amount to $400 a year, or about $33 a month.

After the investor has analyzed all of these factors, the net income (also called "real" or "effective" income) can be found for the property both as it stands and as it will be after it is rehabilitated. The comparative information for a building might be charted as follows, using a four-flat for illustration:

INCOME

Rent Schedule	Seller's Operating Statement	Adjusted Current Estimates	Projected Future Estimates
Apt. 1			
Apt. 2			
Apt. 3			
Apt. 4			
Gross possible rents			
Less vacancies/rent loss			
Total rents, apartments			
Other income (garage rental, laundry, etc.)			
GROSS INCOME			

EXPENSES

	Seller's Operating Statement	Adjusted Current Estimates	Projected Future Estimates
Administrative			
Operating			
Maintenance			
Taxes-insurance			
Services			
Other payroll			
Operating expenses			

HOW MUCH IS IT WORTH? | 43

Replacement reserve _____ _____ _____

TOTAL EXPENSES _____ _____ _____

NET INCOME (Gross income
less total expenses) _____ _____ _____

An investor who has processed income and expenses correctly now possesses the most important single piece of information about an investment property: its net income. From that figure, you can learn several other vital things about the property and the market:

- By a process known as capitalization, you can learn what the sophisticated investment market considers the property to be worth.
- You can determine by adding in the additional costs of mortgage principal and interest payments whether the property will return any cash on the investment—or merely tax benefits and potential appreciation.
- Your projections of income and expenses after rehabilitation should indicate whether it is worthwhile to go ahead with the project.
- Your own analysis of real income and expenses will be useful in negotiating for the property if you decide to buy it.

The integrity of the investor's estimates that lead to net income thus becomes a critical factor in the whole transaction. If your doubts are substantial enough that you might be even 10 percent off, it would be well to check with a property manager who works for a professional management firm that handles property in the area. The fee will be minimal because the property manager should be able to spot obvious miscalculations from experience.

With several operating statements to compare as to numbers and especially percentages and with commonsense adjustments of your own, the adjusted operating statement should be close to the realities of building operating costs.

Just be careful not to overestimate the rents that can be obtained after rehabilitation. Assume that it is not likely they will exceed those of the best rental building in the neighborhood—at least not at first. Somewhere between the best and the worst building is the rent level that you most likely would be able to command, tending toward the higher rents if the rehabilitation is substantial.

It is common for investors to presume that if their rehabilitated units are 20 percent better than everything else available in the neighborhood, 20 percent higher rents can be obtained. This presumption is mistaken. That is because the market sets the rents, not the level of quality of the housing. The market—meaning typical renters—are likely to choose an entire neighborhood that is superior, not just a superior building in a neighborhood that otherwise does not measure up to the competition of other neighborhoods. Therefore, avoid the temptation to set the after-rehab rental goals too high.

USING GROSS AND NET INCOME

You now possess two extremely important pieces of information—the gross income and net operating income. The first evaluation of these data concerns how they relate to each other. The net operating income should represent at least 50 percent of the gross income. That is, all expenses before any mortgage payments should total no more than half of all income. Otherwise, the investor might not be able to cover the principal and interest payments or, at least, to reduce mortgage payments significantly.

To illustrate, assume that gross income for the property comes to $50,000 and net income to $28,000. That means expenses have amounted to $22,000, or about 44 percent, while income has represented the other 56 percent. That is a good ratio.

Now, look at the projected figures after rehabilitation, both for gross and net income. Again, relate them to each other to be sure that rehabilitation will result in an improved return. If it does not, the effort put into rehab may not be worth it. That is, if the ratio of net to gross income is 57 percent before the rehabilitation and only 54 percent afterward, all the work and money you put into the rehab may not pay off.

Usually, though, the dollar amount and the ratio of net to gross income improves after the rents of a successful rehabilitation are taken into account, instead of the rents that currently are applicable.

Next, you want to analyze the dollar amount that will be left after expenses (net income) to determine whether it is sufficient to make mortgage payments. If not, how much will the investor have to come up with each month to amortize the mortgage?

It should be pointed out here that on many investments of this type, the net income *does not cover* the mortgage payments, especially if the investor has been able to get a loan at a high percentage of the value of the property. For these investors, it is adequate that their tenants are helping them pay for a building that someday will sell for a substantially higher price and that meantime will result in tax advantages.

Moreover, many investors occupy one of the units in a building they have purchased for investment. Thus, the rent they would be paying another landlord is subsidized, in effect, as they have to contribute less to the mortgage payment on the property than their tenants, who are paying full market rent.

For example, if the building is a three-flat in which two tenants are paying $240 each, the owner-investor might be able to occupy the identical third unit for only a $120 additional contribution to the total cost of operating the building and paying off its mortgage. Even before tax benefits, that is a $120 saving over what the investor would pay for the same apartment as a renter in the same building.

However, you certainly need to know before you go ahead with a purchase just how you will stand after taking mortgage payments into account. That can be accomplished by use of the standard amortization tables, which are available from banks, libraries, or book stores.

To illustrate, assume that you can obtain an 80 percent loan—meaning the lender will provide 80 percent of the value his appraiser puts on the property. The interest rate is assumed to be 10 percent, and the pay-back period or term of the loan is 20 years. Thus, if you are borrowing $80,000 on a $100,000 property, the loan constant would be eighty times the amount shown in the amortization tables ($9.66) for a 10 percent loan to be repaid over 20 years. That would amount to $772.80 a month.

Here is how to set up your own equation, similar to the above:

Probable price (not the owner's asking price)
at which the property can be purchased   _____

Less downpayment   _____

Amount to be financed   _____

Amount to be financed divided by $1000   _____

At this point, you look in the amortization tables for the interest rate that you expect to pay and number of years in which you have agreed to repay the loan. The figure at the top of these tables indicates what you will pay in interest and principal amounts per $1000 borrowed. Thus, you can take the last number above (amount to be financed divided by $1000) and multiply it by the figure per $1000 from the amortization tables, and precisely figure what you will owe the lender each month in principal and interest on the mortgage needed to buy the property.

Remember that you have already taken into account every other factor of cost to own the property, including taxes and insurance. So by adding the expenses to the monthly payment to amortize the mortgage, you have what should be the sum total of your payout on the building.

Remember too, that while income and expenses likely will change after the building is rehabbed, the principal and interest on the original loan to buy it will remain constant. The only exception would be if you buy the property with one of the new mortgage programs in which the interest rates can be adjusted over the life of the mortgage. This type of loan is still rare, however, and for the purposes of this analysis, only the traditional mortgage plan that is the basis for almost all of the real estate loans in this country will be considered.

DECIDING WHETHER TO BUY

Now you have three figures that tell you whether you should buy the property or not. One is the net income, that amount you have to spend after taking all expenses except the mortgage loan into account. The second is the amount you would expect to spend to cover mortgage payments immediately upon purchasing the property. The third is the net income estimate after rehabilitation. By comparing these figures, the merits of the investigation become clear, as this example will illustrate:

Assume that the following figures have resulted from refinement of the income and expense statement:

Net income when purchased	$24,000 a year divided by 12, or $2000 a month
Net income when rehabbed	$32,000 a year divided by 12, or $2500 a month
Mortgage costs per month	$1800

It may quickly be seen that the property as it stands does not figure to be much of an investment from a cash-return standpoint. However, tax advantages also should be taken into consideration. Most of the $1800 mortgage costs per month can be deducted from other income in the early years of the loan. If $1500 can be so deducted, a taxpayer in the 33 percent tax bracket would realize shelter benefits worth $500. Another taxpayer, this one in the 25 percent bracket, would realize $375 in sheltered income.

Also, it should be emphasized that many people buy property of this type solely for potential appreciation and do not really care whether it produces any cash return or not. They simply speculate that the neighborhood is changing for the better or demand for this type of building is growing, and hold it for sale 2 to 5 years down the road, meanwhile rehabbing the units to increase rents and make it still more valuable.

Others do not intend to make mortgage payments for very long anyway because they are just going to rehab the building and sell it at the earliest possible moment. So, the little cash that it produces in the meantime is irrelevant.

HOW MUCH IS IT WORTH? 47

Whatever the investor's strategy, it is well to make the above calculations in order to decide how much more valuable the real estate would be if rehabilitated. In the example cited, it is $500 a month times 12 months, or $6000, more valuable in terms of return each year to the person who is holding it. Depending on the market, that $6000 may be multiplied six to ten times in value when the property is sold.

That is because investors tend to buy income-producing property on the basis of a multiple of its net or gross income. In fact, newspaper advertisements for buildings of this type often stipulate that the property sells for X times gross income (not to be trusted) or X times net income (a more reliable indicator).

When you analyze a few sales in terms of the net income claimed for them, you can get some handle, though not an entirely reliable one, on how many times net income the market for that area thinks these properties are worth. (By the "market," again, the reference is to what willing buyers will pay willing sellers, neither under any compulsion to buy or sell, in an open-market transaction.)

Appraisers use a more sophisticated approach called the capitalization technique. Because your lender's appraiser will use this approach, it is well to understand it because its implications as to what the lender will allow on the property are of considerable consequence. In fact, you should be prepared for the appraiser to use a higher capitalization rate and thus put a lower value on the property than you might think it is worth.

Here is how that happens: Basically, the capitalization rate is the yield or return on an investment that will attract buyers to that particular investment. Thus, it always exceeds the interest rate that could be realized by simply putting available capital into another, safer vehicle, such as U.S. Treasury bonds. A second element in the capitalization rate is the annual percent of the purchase price that it would take to recover that price over the remaining life of the property.

For example, assume that the safest investments—Treasury notes or AAA bonds—return 7 to 7.5 percent. Investors in real estate, therefore, would look for something better than that, at least 9 percent for the type property that would be subject to rehabilitation. They are getting leverage and tax advantages in addition to a return on investment, but they also are taking a risk that other investments do not require, so the higher return is expected.

But, beyond the return on the investment, buyers of real estate expect to recapture the amount for which they bought the property before it loses value through deterioration. Thus, if the building seems to have at least another 20 years of useful life, the investor would expect by the end of that time to have recovered what he originally put into it. For a 20-year life, the investor would want 5 percent a year in his amortization of the purchase price because 1 year is 5 percent of 20 years. Thus, the capitalization rate in this example would be 9 plus 5 or 14 percent.

Then, it is a formula used by real estate appraisers that the net income divided by the capitalization rate equals market value for the building. Note that the reference here is to the *building* alone, not the land, because the land does not deteriorate. Thus, before using this formula, appraisers deduct the value of the land, then add it back after the formula has been applied to the building separately.

This poses the problem of the estimated value of the land. Brokers and financial institutions are the best source of data on land sales. They will usually quote the price by the foot, and the size of the lot can be multiplied by that figure. But, in practice, 20 percent of the sale price usually is attributed to the land, the other 80 percent to the building.

To show how this whole process works, assume a net income in the previous example of $21,000, with a capitalization rate of 14 percent. The estimated market value of the building would be $21,000 divided by 0.14, or $150,000. That is for the building. Now, add another 20 percent for the land, and the value of the property by the income approach to appraisal would be $180,000.

This exercise has been necessary to acquaint the investor with the way property of this type is usually appraised. But, capitalization rates are not that difficult to discover. Brokers often speak in terms of the figure at which the property would be capitalized. Lenders have a figure that they use in each area, based on their sales data. Moreover, by watching sales of other properties in an area, you can see what capitalization rate was accepted by buyers of similar properties. This is the best evidence of all because it is that trusted "market data" that investors and lenders alike use to place value on property.

Thus, if the above sale occurred at $180,000 for a property that had an expected income of $21,000, then the capitalization rate for the building obviously was 14 percent—the $150,000 value of the building excluding land divided into $21,000 equals 0.14.

The reasons for learning something of the capitalization process instead of merely relying on sales of comparable properties to determine what should be paid for the subject property are twofold:

First, the lender's appraiser will use this rate, and if so much as 1 or 2 percent is added to what the real capitalization rate should be, the value of the property can be significantly reduced in the all-important bank appraisal. By using a 16 percent capitalization rate instead of a 14 percent rate in the above example, the appraiser would have valued the building at $131,000 instead of $150,000. The investor thus would have to come up with $19,000 more to buy the property at its market value. By having evidence of several actual transactions in the area, the investor might persuade the lender that a lower capitalization rate prevails in the market and should be used.

Second, the investor who plans to rehab the property can tell by the projected net income after rehabilitation how much value will be added to the building because of its improvement. Thus, if net income can be expected to rise to $25,000 from $21,000 after rehabilitation and 14 percent is the going capitalization rate, the building's value will be seen to increase from $150,000 ($21,000 divided by 0.14) to more than $178,000 ($25,000 divided by 0.14).

It can be quickly seen from this exercise just how much can be expended for the rehabilitation work without exceeding the value that can be added by the effort. In the example given, the limit on any rehabilitation expenditures would be something under $28,000. Otherwise, the rehabilitation would produce no added value and would be a waste of the investor's time. Especially would this be true for the investor who wanted to sell the property immediately without holding it for potential future appreciation.

These processes may seem time-consuming to the investor, but they are not. They are simple data-gathering, with uncomplicated mathematics to refine the data. If the investor does not seek this information and analyze it in terms of goals, the investment represents mere speculation that may prove to be financially disastrous.

It is really comparable to gathering information about a company in which an investor wants to purchase stock. The price-earnings ratio for a stock can be likened to the capitalization procedure for real estate.

As a stock broker supplies helpful information to the securities investor, so real estate brokers can be the source of much useful data about income-producing real property. But, the real estate broker's data are less based upon fact and must be checked out. Even if an investor engages an appraiser to carry out this analysis, it is well to know as much as possible before buying the appraisal service. Otherwise, the appraisal fee could be wasted on a property that really does not have the characteristics of a good financial return.

Armed with a good supply of market data, the investor can achieve such results as these:

- Determine how realistic the asking price on the property is.
- Decide how high to make the first offer.
- Produce valid figures for negotiation.
- Anticipate future income after the rehabilitation.
- Know the maximum amount that can be spent on the rehabilitation to estimate whether it would really be feasible to upgrade the property.

- Impress lenders that the feasibility of the project has been well analyzed.

This chapter has dealt mostly with several-unit buildings, but it applies as well to a single-family home that is to be purchased for rehabilitation and rental. Data-gathering should merely be concentrated on similar one-unit buildings, rather than on buildings of two or more units. While it is possible to draw valid conclusions from the comparison of units that are alike in anything from a two- to a six-flat, the investor in a one-unit building must compare the property to others of similar size or risk drawing invalid conclusions. That is because buildings with more than one unit share some things in common—the roof, heating system, some walls, the yard, etc. Thus, the expenses for these common elements are shared, as they are not when one tenant occupies an entire building.

How much is it worth, then?

By comparing recent sales of similar properties, by capitalizing the net income now and after rehabilitation, and by learning from the experience of the marketplace, that answer should not be difficult to discover.

4 | BUYING IT FOR LESS

Once having arrived at a well-reasoned judgment as to how much a potential investment is worth, the investor begins the process of trying to buy it for less than that amount by exercising good negotiating techniques.

The first step will be to compare the investor's own estimate of the market value of the property with the asking price. If the difference is no more than 20 percent, a deal should eventually be consummated and, more often than not, closer to the buyer's figure than the seller's. That is because the seller usually has no greatly exaggerated view of his property's value. In many cases, the asking price still represents a neat profit because the owner has held it for several years, after buying it at a significantly lower price.

Too, the seller may not have the vision to see that his property could become a money maker with rehabilitation. All he may know is that the tenants' complaints grow in number, the place seems to eat money in repairs, and the vacancies are harder and harder to fill. He has put the property on the market at a realistic price to stick someone else with those headaches.

The difficulty comes from the other type seller. He thinks real estate prices have been escalating all around his area, so why not for his property too. Therefore, the asking price is much above the market value. It may take several months on the market with no serious buyers to shake that attitude. Sometimes, it is best just to look for other opportunities because the property may never change hands if the owner has other resources and a stubborn streak.

Which brings up the first important point about negotiating: know the seller. Try to find out who the seller is, what the circumstances of the owner are, how much property is owned besides the subject building, and whether there is any urgency to move the property.

If the seller is a veteran of many real estate deals, owner of several buildings, and well-to-do financially, the buyer has a different set of problems than if the seller is an elderly couple ready to flee to the Sun Belt or a new inheritor of the property.

The long-time dealer in the real estate market probably knows exactly how much the property is worth and, usually, will not be persuaded to take less. So, it becomes a matter of whether the property still has potential as a rehabbed building if it is bought at or near full market value before rehabilitation.

Negotiation still would be expected with such an owner because the property is undoubtedly priced well above what it is expected to bring. However, the chances of picking up a bargain are minimized in dealing with such an experienced seller.

On the other hand, few owners of run-down property have such expertise or they would not be sitting on a building that has failed to keep pace with the appreciation in the rest of the real estate market. More often, the seller is a long-time owner, often the occupant of one unit, who thinks of the values of the good old days, when the property might have sold for a fraction of what you are prepared to offer. Sometimes that thinking has been reflected in the rents that such an owner has been asking—another reason the building may be a bargain. (This type owner also offers the opportunity for some creative financing, involving the seller's holding the mortgage, as will be seen in the chapter on financing.)

Another common type of seller of these properties is the widow or descendant of a long-time owner who has died. The family needs to sell in order to pay the taxes on the estate. In these cases, a professional appraiser usually is called in to establish the value of the property, and, if time permits, the new owner often will hold out for something close to this appraisal.

Buyers of investment property rarely will run into one of their own kind selling. That is, the party on the seller's side will not usually be another investor who bought the property mainly for its potential as a profitable investment.

The last price paid for the property is important enough to the negotiations to make a trip to the local registry of deeds to find out. The amount of tax stamps purchased for the deed will indicate the price and the date of the last sale. Only in rare instances will this information be misleading—when a sophisticated buyer has purchased more stamps than necessary as a device to throw off the next purchaser. In most states, it is perfectly legal to buy more tax stamps than needed, but not less. However, in most cases, the buyer purchases only the necessary amount.

How is this information useful? If the owner bought the property ten years ago and inflation has doubled its value despite the deterioration of the physical real estate, a substantial profit awaits the seller, even if the property does not bring its asking price. The seller thus will be less likely to insist on a certain figure. The memory of how little was paid for it, compared to what is being offered, will encourage a seller to take the money and run.

On the other hand, if the property was purchased just 3 years ago and little or no appreciation has occurred, the owner can be assumed to be selling because of a need for the money out of an unprofitable investment. In these cases, so little has been paid to the equity that a favorable mortgage may exist, which can be assumed. It might be worth giving the owner close to the asking price in order to take over the favorable financing if that can be made part of the deal.

It is critical to judging how much negotiating strength a buyer has to decide whether the real estate market in the area is a buyer's or seller's market. The investor should know by researching an area just how rapidly real estate has been turning over. If it typically has taken 3 to 6 months to move a building of this type, you can feel relatively safe in ignoring the broker's insistence that you may lose the property if you do not act immediately. It is still a buyer's market when property is that slow to sell.

On the other hand, if a neighborhood already shows positive momentum and a good property comes along, it is well to be ready to make an offer because you are in a seller's market. But, do not be guided by the broker. The broker will try to convince you that every market is a seller's market and that the time you waste will cost you a chance to buy.

The broker's interest in producing a sale to earn a commission works to your advantage in that the broker is inclined to put almost as much pressure on the seller to come down in price as on the buyer to offer more. Though theoretically working for, and being paid by, the seller, the broker really works to make the sale and earn the commission.

That means the broker will gladly aid in the negotiations by conveying your concerns about such things as the high vacancy in the building, the expense to the buyer to replace the roof or upgrade the heating plant, etc. Then, the broker will try to get the seller to take those factors into account and ask a more "realistic" price so the sale can be consummated, as well as to persuade the seller that you are a good prospect, whose interest in the property should be taken seriously.

But, at some point, the investor will be required to show, by more than the broker's conviction, a serious commitment. That time is when a written offer must be made and a deposit submitted.

There are standard forms for making an offer to buy. They cover most of the legal points that are necessary for the buyer's protection, including items to be prorated, a legal description of the property, the date and place of closing, and liens against the property.

However, the offer to buy should also include any replacement or repairs that the buyer expects the seller to assume as a condition of sale. The offer might also be conditional on the buyer obtaining financing and on approval of the transaction by the buyer's attorney and accountant. Items such as carpeting, appliances, fixtures, and other components that might be taken by the seller should be specified to be conveyed to the buyer as part of the sale.

This is the point at which the buyer should employ an attorney. From the time that an offer to buy comes into the picture, the legal side of buying real estate comes increasingly into play. It pays to have the protection of an experienced real estate attorney (friends and brokers will suggest one) from this point forward.

A word of caution, though, about the attorney: he is your legal counsel, not your real estate counsel. If the attorney is going to represent an investor in negotiating a deal, it is good advice not even to tell the attorney what your top price really is. The attorney who is not spending the money and knows what you actually are willing to pay, might negotiate less skillfully.

Usually, though, negotiations to buy real estate are carried on between a potential buyer and the real estate agent who represents the seller. It does not work well for a potential buyer to try to negotiate directly with an owner-seller. Personality conflict can become part of the process, as it usually does *not* when a third party tries to work out a deal. Also, an owner can develop unexpected pride of ownership and stubbornness when someone starts downgrading his property, as the prospective buyer must do. When the downgrading comes through a broker, it is diluted and indirect, and cannot be taken as an insult.

However, it is well to give the negotiating agent some reason for offering so much less than a seller might ask. Without being too specific, an investor can mention high vacancy in the area and in the building, the run-down condition of the heating system that will require early expense to a new owner, the higher capitalization rates that are common in the area compared to the subject property, or anything else that applies.

The owner, upon hearing solid reasons such as these, knows that the money —at least yours—is not just going to be stolen and will often make a major concession on the price right at the beginning of the negotiations.

That is when most of the big concessions are made—at the beginning of negotiations. The seller's first response to a written offer that is well below asking price should be a substantial reduction in the original figure, or the negotiations are likely to be difficult.

But, the investor should avoid making a first offer that insults the seller. The essence of negotiation is the compromise of interests that are not impossibly diverse. Offering $40,000 for a property that you know to be worth $70,000 and that is being advertised for $80,000 can have the effect of just riling the owner and making serious negotiation impossible. But, by offering 20 percent less than the $70,000 that you think it is worth, or $56,000, you have established a basis for negotiating to buy the property without angering or upsetting the seller.

The amount of the first offer is a key to the negotiations. Experienced buyers start at a figure 20 to 25 percent under market value or under the amount they eventually would be willing to pay. Take a look at that percentage. It leaves plenty of room for maneuver as negotiations continue, yet is not so far from reality that it should be unrealistic to the seller.

The importance of putting this offer in writing should be fully understood. If it is in writing, with a deposit of $500 to $1000 (whatever is customary in the area), it has to be taken seriously. Furthermore, if the building is owned by more than one person, a written offer must be submitted to all owners. In the case of a family that has inherited the real estate, different needs may be involved within the ownership group. Some may want to sell the property in a hurry, and they might overrule other relatives who want to wait for the top dollar. If the offer is written, the negotiator for the family is compelled to show it to the entire ownership group, some of which may say, "Sell it."

The investor should not think only of price as the area in which concessions can be made that will bring about an advantageous agreement. Often, the prospective buyer can offer the seller something more important than a few thousand additional dollars.

For example, a seller sometimes has as much concern about the timing of the sale as about the price. There may be a tax deadline, or the sale of the subject property may be important to the purchase of another property. The latter often is the case when elderly sellers are involved. They may be purchasing a home in the Sun Belt that they need the cash from their old building to consummate.

If you are in a position to do so, tell the negotiator that you are able to accommodate the seller as to the date of sale if the haggling over price can be minimized or ended. Sometimes, the seller will decide, "Okay, if I can get the money in 2 weeks, I'll take it."

Another form of concession involves items that the owner may want included in a sale that the investor previously has excluded. The seller may, for example, have no use for outdoor equipment—a lawnmower, snowblower, etc.—because of moving into a condominium. By offering additional cash for those items, the prospective buyer may obtain some useful equipment, while making the seller more receptive to a lower offer on the building.

The investor may also find it beneficial to negotiations to back off from some original demands that the owner make certain repairs as a condition of sale. Suppose, for example, that the letter of intent to buy stipulates that the seller must replace several broken windowpanes.

That may seem a small matter and hardly worth any concession in price. But, the owner may be absent and unable to deal with it or, more likely, will simply want no more expense or involvement with the property—just to sell it and be rid of it. In such a case, the hassle of finding someone to replace the broken glass may be magnified until it seems a bigger problem than it is.

The important thing to remember in negotiating, then, is to consider all factors, not just the price. Give the seller something, and you usually will get something in return.

There are times, though, when it is a waste to continue to negotiate; the deal just is not going to be made.

One of those times is when the seller will not budge from too high a price. Do not get so committed to a property that you cannot walk away from it in these circumstances. Some property is put on the market at a price that is far out of line with the real world, just on the owner's hope that some sucker will come along and buy it at that price. Otherwise, this type seller is not interested in making a deal. The seller is just trolling to see if any fish will grab the hook.

This type owner can be spotted first by the high asking price, and second by an unwillingness to come down to any reasonable extent when a respectable offer is made. Ask this owner's broker how long—and how often—this property has been offered at this price. It may have been sitting there for a year at the same level. When an owner has had a property on the market for a year without lowering the price to try to attract buyers, it is obvious what game is being played. Not a game in which an intelligent investor would want to participate.

On the other hand, an owner can simply be duped by friends and articles about real estate trends into thinking that the property has considerably more value than it does. Then, further negotiations may be in order because the broker will soon convince the owner of the folly of such an asking price after a few prospects have seen the building and declared it overpriced.

Stick close to your first offer if you see this educational process occurring and have the time to wait. Remind the broker, who will remind the seller, that you have a standing offer when they are ready to negotiate realistically. The broker is your best ally in this situation and will keep referring the seller back to the sure thing—and the sure commission—that you represent. In fact, the broker will soon suggest the real price that would buy the property as the seller begins to weaken. Then, you can consider whether to raise your offer to that level, or near it.

But, the broker will also work *on you,* the buyer, by talking about other prospects and the offers they are prepared to make if you do not move fast. In some cases, the broker will even show you a signed contract for a higher price than your offer. Be skeptical about such contracts. Anybody can write up an offer to buy. If there is a higher offer, why doesn't the seller accept it? Ask the broker, and see how plausible the response is.

You can play this game too. In fact, it is always good strategy to know about a second building, or a third, that is almost as good as the one you really want to buy. It is especially good if the alternate building is handled by another broker. That stirs the broker for the building you really want to put much more pressure on the owner to take your offer.

Negotiating is a difficult and tricky business. But, the rewards justify paying a lot of attention to it. When you can purchase a $100,000 building for $90,000, you already know that you have a $10,000 profit. And, when you also know that, after rehabilitation, that building will be worth $125,000, then you are looking at the kind of profits that rehabbing can bring. The $10,000 you have saved upfront may pay for the whole rehab effort and leave $25,000 as pure profit.

Some rehabbers will not buy a building unless they can get that kind of bargain. They will just await the next opportunity. Such patience is a great thing, but it may not be feasible for the first-time rehab investor. When the right building comes along that seems to offer the good prospect of a buy at less than market value, it is advisable to negotiate for it, without getting so committed that it would be heartbreaking not to be able to buy.

5 | HOW DO YOU FINANCE IT?

The essential strategy of any real estate investment should be to borrow as much money as the property will allow and let someone else pay it back.

It is called financing with leverage, and it is the main thing that makes real estate investment so attractive. So little of the capital needed to buy real estate comes out of the investor's own pocket, compared to the value of the property acquired, that the profit potential per dollar invested can be much greater than can be realized in other types of investment. Moreover, an investor in income-producing property can so arrange the financing of the purchase that the tenants pay enough in rents to cover all, or at least a substantial part of, the monthly cost of borrowing the money.

The investor in this happy position merely collects from one group and pays another, having little or no commitment of funds beyond what was originally necessary to obtain the property—namely, the downpayment, certain fees connected with the securing of a loan, and some minor costs of assuring the title to the property and the legality of the sale.

In a typical real estate transaction, the lender appraises the real estate that is being offered as security for the loan and offers an amount of money equal to some percentage of that appraised value. Usually, it is not 100 percent. More often, the lender will seek some margin in case the borrower cannot meet payments and the property must be sold in foreclosure to obtain a return of the borrowed funds.

The lender's margin is likely to be 20 to 30 percent on an income-producing property. That means the borrower must come up with 20 to 30 percent to get the rest of the money needed to buy the property. But, consider that the investor in government bonds must come up with 100 percent of the investment. To buy stocks and corporate bonds, the investor must supply at least 60 to 80 percent of the necessary capital.

Thus, an investor who realizes a 10 percent return on each type of investment comes out far ahead on real estate. To illustrate, assume a $100,000 asset with a 10 percent return in these investment categories: real estate with a 20 percent downpayment, government bonds with a 100 percent commitment, and stocks with a 70 percent commitment of the investor's own funds.

- The purchaser of real estate in these circumstances realizes a $10,000 annual profit on a commitment of $20,000 of personal funds.
- The purchaser of government bonds realizes $10,000 (actually slightly more because of compounding) on a real dollar commitment of $100,000.
- The purchaser of stock yielding 10 percent gains $10,000 a year on a commitment of $70,000.

That is what leveraging is all about. The real estate investor figures to get half the invested dollars back in 1 year with a 10 percent return on the total value of the property controlled. That does not take into account the tax advantages and potential for appreciation.

Obviously, then, the best investment is one in which the investor has the least amount of personal funds in property that generates the highest yield.

FINDING THE DOWNPAYMENT

That means seeking the lowest downpayment that a lender will allow. The ideal situation would be for the lender to provide all of the cost of buying and rehabilitating a building that yields 10 percent after all expenses and mortgage repayment costs are covered. That goal may not be attainable, but the investor should try to come as close to it as possible.

In a rehabilitation project, the investor may be asked for a downpayment on three occasions: first, in obtaining the money to buy the building; next, in securing the funds to rehabilitate it; and finally, in obtaining the higher loan that will cover the increased value of the property after it has been rehabilitated.

The investor should begin to think of how to finance a rehab plan as soon as it is decided to make this type of investment. The first thing to examine carefully is how to come up with the downpayment. The second is how to persuade the seller, the government, or the lending institution to take as little money down as possible.

Many potential real estate investors are stymied in getting into the field by their lack of funds to meet the initial requirements of lenders for an upfront commitment of their own funds. However, many have resources they do not know they have, which could be tapped to deliver the necessary funds.

For example, many people own homes that have appreciated in value so that they are worth much more than they were when the mortgage on them was written. The difference between the amount of that mortgage and the current value of the property can be extracted by the rather simple process of refinancing.

Refinancing is not recommended when a low interest rate of some previous period is replaced with a significantly higher interest rate today. That is, it is not recommended unless the dollars could be put into a more profitable investment. Then it is a matter of trading an additional 2 to 4 percent interest for an opportunity to realize a great deal more—as in the case of a good real estate investment.

It has been shown that a $20,000 commitment to buy property worth $100,000 can return $10,000 if the property yields 10 percent. That is a much better place to have your money than in the unrealized gain in value of a home. Therefore, if other routes to a downpayment fail, consider refinancing a home. The lender will be glad to accommodate if the change from one mortgage to another involves a higher interest rate.

Remember that in a refinance situation, the homeowner must face higher monthly loan payments. But the higher amount of interest can be deducted from income taxes and reduce the real cost to the borrower.

One cheaper alternative to acquiring the downpayment is to borrow against life insurance, and another may be to borrow from a credit union. Each typically charges less interest than a bank, and security usually is not necessary. The insurance company considers the value of the policy to be adequate security, and the credit union may simply loan money against your employment at a good salary at a company that the credit union serves.

Many investors obtain the downpayment for their first investment from family members or close acquaintances, sometimes with a written agreement to allow those persons to share in the proceeds of a profitable sale or in the interim profits. Any kind of contract can be written to benefit an individual who agrees to loan the money to buy a building for rehabilitation. The following are examples.

More Attractive Interest Rate

The loan can simply be made at an interest rate more attractive than the individual could get through other investments. The borrower does not need the money for long and can afford to pay above the market interest for a short term—until the building is successfully rehabbed and financed at its after-rehab value.

To illustrate, assume that the investor wants to purchase a building for $80,000, with plans to put $10,000 into upgrading it. The increased rents that will result would convince a savings and loan association after the rehab to appraise the property at $110,000. If the investor borrowed 20 percent of the $80,000 needed to buy the building originally, and half the $10,000 rehab cost—$16,000 plus $5,000, or $21,000—almost all of this amount could be recovered and repaid when the permanent mortgage on the $110,000 value is written.

Higher-than-market interest rates should only be used for the short term, however. In raising the downpayment for the permanent mortgage, every effort should be made to hold the interest paid at no higher than the going rate for second mortgages—usually three points above the rate for first mortgages.

Share Profits of a Rehab Project

An offer to share in the rewards of a rehab project can be contracted with a partner. Often, a relative or friend is looking for some way to get into real estate investment. If your projections of profit are so defensible that *you* are anxious to go ahead with a purchase, they should be persuasive to a possible investment partner—especially a partner who would not be able or willing to go through the process of rehab personally.

Partners of this type are especially easy to convince if your plans involve fixing up the property for immediate resale. They know it will be just a matter of months before their investment is repaid, with a solid profit as well.

Here is how such a deal can be structured: Assume that the investment partner is willing to advance $9000 toward the purchase and rehabilitation of a $60,000 two-flat. The investor puts up another $9000 and buys the building for $12,000 down on a conventional 80 percent loan. The extra $6000 covers the rehab costs. After the rehab, the higher rentals assure another investor that earnings will be significantly increased and the property would be worth $75,000 in the market. A sale is consummated at that price and the investor nets $9000 ($15,000 less rehab costs) plus the $9000 borrowed previously. That amount can be paid back with some percentage of the gain, perhaps 20 percent, or $1800, added. The investor still has netted $7200 on a mere $9000 commitment. (Various costs of obtaining the loan and paying interest would reduce the gain somewhat.)

HOW DO YOU FINANCE IT? 63

Broker or Broker's Client Participation

If the investor knows no personal or business acquaintance who might want to participate in such a plan, ask the real estate broker. Maybe the broker will even put personal funds in the deal. After all, two commissions are at stake, one when the building is sold as is, the other when it is sold again after rehabbing. If the broker believes in the area, and thinks you know what you are doing, the broker may either take part in the deal personally or suggest it to other clients.

A real estate broker is aware of clients who have recently made a nice sum of money by selling a home. These sellers often look for some better place to put that money than the bank. Since they recently have been blessed by a gain on a real estate investment, they will often be in the mood to try another. At least the broker can inquire and put the two of you together to see what can be worked out.

Seller Participation

By all means, consider the seller. In fact, as will be seen later in this chapter, the seller should be the first target to finance the entire project. But, you should also start looking there for the downpayment. Many sellers do not need a big cash return. They would prefer a steady income from the property without having the burden of owning it. Therefore, they will listen to offers to buy their buildings on a monthly or annual payment schedule, especially if there are tax advantages. In most cases, there are.

Perhaps the seller has obtained the property through a death or divorce. He or she wants to be rid of the taxes and the rent collections and the whole set of responsibilities of owning an income-producing building. The offer of steady income can be very appealing to such a person. Ask the seller if your accountant can develop some figures that will show it can be beneficial to receive the downpayment over a period of years instead of in a lump sum. Usually, an accountant can find a way to do just that.

Any seller will listen to a deal that involves both immediate and long-term benefits. An immediate benefit that can be offered is a price higher than the seller really expected to get. Thus, to achieve the goal of minimum cash in the purchase, the investor may sacrifice the last few thousand dollars in the negotiations on the stipulation that little or no downpayment will be required.

To illustrate, suppose the buyer's offer is $60,000, and the seller, after some negotiations, is down from an original $70,000 to $65,000, with some evidence of hardening. The investor knows the property is probably worth $64,000, but has been trying to purchase it below the market value. Offer the $64,000 if the seller would be willing to take no money down or just enough money down to cover the real estate agent's commission. Often, a deal can be worked out in such circumstances.

The stumbling block in many cases of this type is *the broker's commission.* The seller does not want any expense. So, the investor who can come up with enough to pay the 6 to 7 percent broker's commission on the sale will be in a stronger position to bargain about the downpayment. A seller finds a deal much more interesting when no dollars have to be paid out. Thus, the seller might consider an amount that also covers the seller's legal costs and other miscellaneous closing expenses in return for 90 percent or better financing. By putting down only the 6 to 7 percent broker's commission and another 1 or 2 percent for other fees, the investor is getting a very high percentage loan that probably would not be available through conventional lending sources. The seller has no expenses and begins almost immediately to receive a monthly check that is approximately equal to the rents formerly collected from the building, with no effort involved and no expenses to worry about. Taxes on the sale of the building are paid on an annual basis, rather than on a lump-sum gain by the seller. It is a good deal for both parties.

Assuming the Seller's Loan

Sometimes, it is not just to reduce or eliminate any cash downpayment by the buyer, but to assume an attractive loan that motivates investors to seek other capital. For example, if the seller has an assumable loan at a low 7 percent interest rate amounting to $30,000 of the $60,000 value of the property, the investor should seek every possible way to keep that mortgage intact. The difference in monthly payments on a 30-year loan at 7 percent and 10 percent is the difference between $6.65 and $8.78 per $1000, or $2.13 per $1000. For a $30,000 loan that can be assumed at 7 percent, the buyer can save thirty times $2.13 or $63.90 a month—$766.80 a year.

It is worth trying to accomplish if the interest on the loan that bridges the gap is not so great that it wipes out the gain. Thus, if the investor must pay 12 percent for some or all of the $30,000 needed to keep the 6 percent loan on $30,000 of a $60,000 price intact, it may not be worth it. An accountant can figure it out and take into account the higher interest deductions in financing the whole property at 10 percent, as opposed to paying 7 percent on part of the price and 10 or 12 percent on the rest.

Again, the seller is the source to look for in obtaining the extra funds to assume a low-interest loan. The seller knows a valuable selling point in the attractive mortgage, and probably will be agreeable to creative financing involving that mortgage.

Suppose, for example, that the investor can only come up with $10,000 toward a $60,000 property on which a 7 percent mortgage is outstanding in the amount of $30,000. Will the seller hold a note for the missing $20,000? Ask and you will often receive.

The advantages to the seller are many. First, the sum immediately received amounts to $30,000 instead of $60,000, so the government will receive less in capital gains tax. Secondly, the $20,000 that the seller permits the buyer to carry over a period of time produces good income at a high rate of interest, probably something above the best rate that government bonds would pay.

The seller also has great safety in his investment because the property is worth $60,000 if foreclosure is necessary and $10,000 has already been paid in the downpayment. If the contract is written that way, the seller gains additional protection by being able to simply resume payments on the original mortgage in case the investor defaults. Thus, if the property cannot be maintained by the investor, the seller can simply take it back, pick up the mortgage, and pocket the $10,000.

It can be seen that in many cases, the seller benefits by helping a buyer with the downpayment. That is why there has been such heavy emphasis in this book on finding out the seller's circumstances in pursuing a rehab investment. The seller may never have realized what additional profit potential the property could have. It is up to the imaginative buyer to offer tempting good ideas that benefit both parties.

Obviously, the investor's advantages are as great as the seller's. Using the seller's money instead of one's own, obtaining a low-interest loan for part of the amount needed to buy, avoiding closing costs, setting up payment terms that work better, and obtaining the best tax arrangement—all are motives to work something out with the seller.

The Land Contract

An additional way to buy a building with little or no downpayment is to utilize a device known as a land contract. In this plan, the seller or some other party retains the deed to the property until it is paid off in full. The buyer has full privileges of possession, but legally does not own the property since the deed has not been transferred.

In other types of real estate purchases, the buyer gets full title to the property, including a deed that legally verifies ownership. The buyer in a land contract makes regular payments to the holder of the deed—usually on a monthly basis just like a mortgage payment—and those payments are credited toward the purchase price. Eventually, the property is paid for and the buyer receives a deed.

What troubles many buyers about a contract sale is that most contracts are written so that a default by the buyer for even 30 to 90 days (depending on the state law) can mean losing all the money paid toward the property. Thus, a buyer may have made payments for 10 years toward a building and have reduced the remaining principal substantially and then might miss a payment or two. The holder of the deed could declare the contract forfeited and take the property back without any reimbursement to the buyer.

But, contracts offer several advantages that the investor should consider. First, there is the likelihood of a reduced downpayment. A seller will usually require very little down if a land contract is acceptable. The seller obviously does not need the money immediately or would demand that the buyer obtain a conventional mortgage.

Especially would the seller be likely to cooperate on a lower downpayment if such cooperation were rewarded by a better price for the property. By giving the seller the full market value or slightly more, the buyer can bargain for a downpayment that would be minimal or nonexistent.

A contract with the seller also enables the buyer to retain a favorable interest rate on the seller's loan, if such a situation exists. In this case, the deal is structured so the buyer makes payments on the loan through the seller, and the difference is made up by contract payments.

To illustrate, suppose a property worth $80,000 has a mortgage with 10 years remaining at an interest rate of 6 percent. But, the mortgage only represents $20,000 of the $80,000 price. The investor then offers to establish a contract in which the seller would continue to pay off the loan, giving the investor the advantage of the 6 percent interest on that amount.

The remaining $60,000 note would be held by the seller and paid off at the going interest rate or perhaps a point or two above the going rate. Because part of the debt would be paid at such a low rate of interest, the investor could afford to offer more interest on the $60,000, making the deal even more attractive to the seller.

The contract can be one way to get around a lending institution that will not allow a loan assumption. These lenders stipulate in mortgages that in the event of a sale, the loan must be paid off in full. But, a contract is not considered a sale in the legal sense because the deed has not actually changed hands through an exchange of money. Recently, some lenders have recognized this matter and started writing new mortgage terms that provide that a contract will be recognized as equivalent to a sale. But, it is unlikely that an old mortgage at a low rate of interest would have that stipulation.

HOW DO YOU FINANCE IT?

Even if the seller needs a big immediate cash sum out of the property, a contract purchase can be arranged to the satisfaction of both parties. That result can be accomplished if the seller just refinances and then sells to the investor on a contract basis.

Consider this example: The seller of the $60,000 building needs $18,000 to buy a house. The current mortgage is paid down to $25,000, and the seller wants to get rid of the problems of ownership of the building. The investor suggests that the seller refinance—take out a new mortgage at 80 percent of $60,000, or $48,000. The $25,000 balance on the old loan would be paid off, and the seller would end up with $23,000.

Part of that would go to the broker as a commission, which would have to be paid in the event of a sale also, and part to the lending institution and other participants in the closing on a new loan. But, the seller would have $18,000 in cash. The loan would then be paid off by the investor on a contract basis.

For the investor, the advantage would be a 100 percent loan because the seller would not need a downpayment anymore to get the $18,000 cash needed. The mortgage would be held and paid off by the seller at the same rate that the buyer would have paid if the buyer had taken out a mortgage on the same property. The investor has saved cash to use in the rehabilitation and let the seller produce the mortgage.

The seller might also be attracted by the idea of a shorter mortgage or contract term—perhaps 10 years instead of 25. That would mean huge cash payments each month by the investor until the property was sold or paid off. But, the idea of receiving such income—much greater than had been available when the seller owned and rented out the building—would appeal to many property owners.

As an example, assume that the investor, only planning to hold the building for 2 or 3 years, suggests that the seller accept a 10-year note, payable in monthly sums of $800. The seller, who has only been receiving $400 a month in rent from the property, now has a chance to get double that amount and to not have to deal with the problems of owning a rental building any longer. Will the seller waive the downpayment and accept that kind of deal? In many cases, yes.

The investor in this case knows that the $800-a-month payments will be tough to produce for the length of time of holding the property. But, instead of having to come up with 20 percent down, the investor just has to meet the monthly payments. If the building is improved so that it brings in $600 in rents instead of $400, there will only be out-of-pocket costs of $200 a month. For many people with good incomes but little savings, this might be a way to go.

Think creatively about involving the seller in your financing. Force the broker to think along with you. The investor in rehab property wants to avoid putting much money down on the original purchase of the building so it can be concentrated on the rehab process. After the building is rehabbed, the investor can look again at the terms under which money was borrowed to get the building. As will be seen, better financing should then be considered, and a lending institution will be more amenable to handling the whole improved package.

The seller, it should be emphasized, is not the only potential source for a contract agreement. Other investors with funds to put into a well-secured loan would find a contract to be a worthwhile investment, returning a monthly cash amount at a healthy rate of interest with little risk if the buyer defaults. The broker might know such people or might take on that type investment personally. Consider rich relatives or friends too. It is a good deal for them.

A contract should be written so that it can be paid off any time or transferred. Often, an investor will want to rehabilitate a property, rent it for a while, and then sell at the appreciated value. It is handy then to tell a prospective buyer that a contract can be assumed, as an alternative to taking out a full loan.

Government Financing

An important source of low-downpayment financing is the government. Most cities have some kind of program that involves federal or nonprofit funding for rehabilitation. They usually target a specific neighborhood and offer such incentives as low or no downpayment to persuade people to buy and rehabilitate buildings there. It is a way to fight urban decay that has been adopted effectively in enough instances to have become a strong favorite of municipal governments.

The problem with using these programs is that the neighborhoods specified may have gone beyond the capacity of private investors to turn them around. They may also pose severe security problems.

However, around the edges of some of these areas, investors may be actively moving in. If you see sure signs of such a trend—more definite signs than in better-located neighborhoods—then it would be wise to check out the financing incentives that the local government is offering to attract such interest.

It should also be emphasized that almost all programs that involve government funding require that the investor occupy one unit of the building. The goal of the programs is to increase ownership by people who will commit themselves to living in the neighborhood, rather than just renting their property. Thus, an investor who plans to live elsewhere than in the building being rehabbed would not qualify under some programs.

At any rate, it pays to check with a city or county housing or planning department. Also, look for an organization known as Neighborhood Housing Services, which in many cities makes loans when bank financing is difficult to find. NHS is a coalition of private and public sources that work on a nonprofit basis to revitalize deteriorating neighborhoods.

Most major cities in the United States offer special programs in rehabilitation, and the eligibility requirements for each, downpayment, interest rate, and other pertinent information will be indicated in the following section.

"BARGAIN-HUNTING" WITH GOVERNMENT PROGRAMS

The federal government and individual community governments encourage rehabilitation by offering programs that provide low-interest loans or the opportunity to buy property at a bargain price. The concept of these programs is to provide incentives to invest in certain designated neighborhoods so that private investors will be willing to help arrest deteriorating conditions by putting time and money into the property. In most programs, an investor also is expected to live in the building rather than rent it to others and live elsewhere.

Dangers exist for the potential investor in these properties because the blight may be irreversible. Also, security problems may make the area hazardous both for the investor and the rehab laborers. Finally, when the property is ready to be marketed for sale or rental, it may be difficult to convince would-be buyers or tenants that the area is a safe place to live.

Therefore, it is critical for the profit-motivated investor to take a careful look at the neighborhood from a standpoint of its dangerous influences, police protection, and pattern of crime and punishment before going into one of the "designated" city areas for rehabilitation. It may be that the bargain price of the real estate or the loan is no bargain when considered with the crime record of the area.

The first thing an investor considering a government program should do is tour the area to see if other investors are taking the same chance you would take. The signs should be obvious if they are taking such risks: building permits will abound, or at least be distinctly evident. Rehabbers like you will have their contractors or subcontractors on the job. In the best of circumstances, some finished rehab projects will be there for the viewing, and for evaluation as to whether they attracted renters or new owners after rehab.

It also pays to visit the police precinct or central police headquarters. Get crime data that are compiled for the area, and note any trends that indicate a worsening or improvement in the area, as measured by crime statistics. Ask the police personnel what the principal sources of crime have been in the area, and whether the type of criminal activity is property damage, personal assault, or simple burglary, purse-snatching, or less serious crimes.

No matter how desirable the financial terms may be on a building, it makes no sense to enter a situation where the police have virtually abandoned the protection of property—as is the case in areas of some cities. Nor would it be reasonable to hope for a turnaround when many incidents of personal assault are part of the criminal record for an area. Lesser crimes indicate that the neighborhood could be salvaged if the police still patrol regularly and respond promptly to calls.

The best sources to ask about these matters are the commercial owners and tenants in the area. They have more valuable merchandise to be burglarized, and would be the prime targets, ahead of residential property owners.

Therefore, talk to merchants in the area, and see what their experience has been. Ask if the police protection is deteriorating or improving. If it is still in decline, forget the whole idea and look for a neighborhood where there is little or no problem with personal security or extreme vandalism.

Some of these "designated" areas offer good profit potential, however, so government programs should not be ignored. For example, a designated area may be the next neighborhood beyond other areas that are undergoing massive rehabilitation. They may offer bargains compared to what is still available in the neighborhood where rehab action already is well along. And, they may be the logical next move for persons anxious to get in on that action, but who can't afford to buy the now-inflated prices in the "hot" area nearby.

The signs again should be evaluated carefully as to whether it is realistic that the rehab movement will continue into the next adjoining neighborhood. If there is some natural barrier between two such neighborhoods—a river, rail tracks, or a highway, for example—the progress toward the new area may stop because it is difficult for the market to bridge such physical barriers. But, if there is no good reason why the strength of one neighborhood should not extend into an adjoining one, see if the government has some program there that might bring a low-interest loan or a favorable price on the property there.

Municipal governments usually administer all government rehab programs, even those funded by the federal government. Therefore, the first place to seek advice about government programs is the local government's housing, planning, or community development office. (Different offices handle rehab programs in each city.)

The first program the investor will encounter in almost any city is the federal loan program known as Section 312. This plan offers low-interest (3 percent in early 1980) mortgages on property in a designated area, with up to 20 years to repay the money. It is possible to borrow up to $27,000 per dwelling unit to cover the cost of rehabilitation and related costs. Both single-family and multifamily buildings are eligible.

In this program, credit might be established through a similar process as that required by a financial institution. There are no income limits, meaning that your annual income need not be below a certain level as in some programs that are intended to help low-income buyers of property.

The federal government is often in the process of providing other incentives to rehabilitation, believing that it is a way to stop the deterioration of inner urban areas. Therefore, it would pay the rehab investor to call the nearest Federal Housing Administration office to see what legislation Congress has recently approved that might be a source of cheap financing for low-cost housing.

By low-cost housing, the government really means *low cost.* In fact, the figure may be as low as $1 as the Federal Housing Administration tries to unload properties it has had to take back, for which there is no market.

People prepared to take the risk of rehabbing a property that usually has been vandalized and stripped down to a shell can consider such investments. This book does not recommend that program. Property that the government considers virtually worthless is usually exactly that—at least, for the profit-minded investor.

Local governments have similar reasons for wanting certain neighborhoods upgraded and for trying to reverse the trend in other neighborhoods that seem to be going downhill. Therefore, they often make rehabilitation funds available just to bring buildings in an area, or in the whole city, back to building code standards.

Thus, if the investor sees the opportunity to buy a good building that has not been kept up to building code requirements, it may be possible to get low-interest loans to bring it back to specifications.

Often, however, these loans are tied to income levels and family sizes. That means that a single investor with no family dependents might be required to put up 10 to 40 percent of the loan amount as a down payment, while a person with five dependents would not be required to put anything down.

The government, in these programs, first wants to help the person with a large family who needs housing. Next, they want to help the person who does not have a high enough income to qualify for a loan from a conventional lender (for example, a savings and loan association).

Remember always in considering these programs that the government has a very different motive than helping you get a property that you can rehab and profit by. The idea behind the legislation that initiates these programs is that given just enough incentive, an investor will consider an otherwise unlikely situation. More important to the authors of these programs than the investment-minded rehabber, though, is the person who will invest hard work in a project with a long-term commitment to live on the premises for the purpose of shelter, not profit.

Therefore, look closely at each program that a community offers. Ask yourself:

- Do I want to live in the building? Most of these programs require the owner to live on the property, rather than to operate it as an absentee landlord. The feeling you have about the security of the neighborhood will be crucial to this decision.
- Am I eligible under the income levels prescribed? Some programs require that the buyer of the program have an income level under local average. You may make more than the average worker in the community and thus be ineligible.
- Is the area that interests me eligible for the federal or local program? Get the exact boundaries before you go any further, because a property that seems feasible for government-aided rehab may be outside the area that is designated.
- Most important of all, especially with the federal Section 312 program, is how long it will take to process an application and get going on a property. Sometimes, the federal government waits so long to approve an application that the property is sold to someone else and all the time and effort put into qualifying go to waste.

The government has many programs to offer, most with admirable goals. However, it is vital to the profit-minded investor that those admirable goals be considered for what they are: incentives for the low-income buyer, or for the person who is willing to take a chance at getting something for almost nothing and will make a serious commitment for a reward that may or may not ever be attained.

Extreme caution is advised before participating in government programs that may be written specifically to exclude the profit that a rehab investor seeks.

DEALING WITH THE LENDER

An investor in a rehab project has three things to finance:

1. The as-is building
2. The cost of materials and labor for rehabilitation
3. The property after rehabilitation when it has become a more valuable building

HOW DO YOU FINANCE IT? 73

The best ways to go about financing these three items are these:

- Buy the as-in building for as little down as possible and spend your available cash on the rehabilitation job.
- Buy the as-is building with a conventional mortgage and use cash to rehab the property as cash becomes available.
- Arrange a loan commitment on the building as it will be after it has been rehabbed and use that commitment to obtain a short-term loan to buy the building and rehabilitate it. The short-term loan is paid off when the building is rehabbed and the "permanent" or "end" loan becomes available. The terms "permanent" and "end" mean the long-term (usually 20 to 30 years) loan that will be needed when the property's new, higher value can be seen by an appraiser who looks at it after it has been improved.

Which of these choices to select depends on whether you plan to sell the building immediately after it is rehabilitated or hold onto it as a rental property until it has appreciated sufficiently to make a sale more attractive.

The prospect of a quick sale obviously means there is no need for a permanent loan. Therefore, what you want to accomplish is the financing of the building as it stands plus the rehabilitation costs. It is rare and unlikely that both can be financed by one institution in one loan without the promise of a permanent loan to pay off the construction and original purchase lenders.

DEALING WITH THE LENDER

Buying the building with as little downpayment as possible has been previously discussed. However, it may be necessary to take out a conventional mortgage with 20 to 30 percent down if better terms cannot be worked out.

Lenders in depressed areas where these properties are located have been accused in the past of refusing to make loans in certain neighborhoods—a practice called "redlining." However, intense public pressure has forced most lenders to agree to offer mortgages in these areas, especially if the buyer is creditworthy and plans to improve the property.

If you run into a case where the lender obviously has no interest in making a loan, ask if there is a procedure available to review your application. Savings and loan associations in many cities have formed committees of public and private citizens to review loan applications where an issue has been raised concerning a charge of redlining.

But, you should be investing in an area where others have already secured loans. As this book previously advised, the first-time investor in a rehab project should not be the pioneer in a new neighborhood. Therefore, find out who financed other properties that are already being rehabbed. The same lender is likely to favor loans to others who will help rehabilitate an area where previous loan commitments have been made.

It is not necessary to advise the lender in this situation that you plan to rehabilitate the building and sell it quickly. Just be sure the loan can be repaid in full without any penalty. If the lender insists on a penalty or requires that no more than a certain percentage of the loan be repaid in one year (30 percent is common), then it will be necessary to explain what is planned and find out what terms can be arranged on a short-term basis.

That should not be fatal to obtaining a loan. But, the lender will ask a higher interest rate than a conventional mortgage would carry under other circumstances.

After buying the building, you will need money to finance the rehabilitation. That is the easy part. There are plenty of property improvement loans at low interest available with government backing. Banks happily provide property improvement loans, though they may charge somewhat higher interest rates than a government guaranteed loan.

Typical of loans insured by the Federal Housing Administration are these:

Type of Improvement	Maximum Maturity	Maximum Amount
Repairs, alterations, or improvements that substantially protect the basic livability or utility of existing structures	12 years	$10,000
Alteration, repair, improvement, or conversion of existing structure used or to be used as a dwelling for two or more families	12 years	$5,000 per dwelling unit

These loans, however, require that the applicant live in the building, so they would not be appropriate for an investor who plans to rehab but never live on the property.

Other property improvement loans are offered by lending institutions with little or no downpayment if the property is not fully mortgaged. That is, if the owner has obtained a conventional 80 percent loan, the property improvement lender may not demand additional collateral.

The going interest rate at the time of this writing, for both FHA-insured and standard property improvement loans, was 12 to 13 percent. However, banks typically charge higher interest for a short-term loan, such as 1 year, than for a 5-year loan.

A typical schedule might be that of a large midwestern savings and loan association. To borrow $5000 for 1 year, the borrower pays 13.62 percent. If the loan is extended over 5 years, the interest rate is 12.53 percent. For 15 years, the interest is collected at only a 10.96 percent rate. The lender wants the in-and-out borrower to pay a premium for money used for such a short duration, while it will settle for less interest from a borrower who will continue to pay for the money for years.

Credit unions and accumulated value in life insurance would be cheaper ways to go. They will charge interest below what any bank would permit, and can be paid back at the borrower's convenience.

If the buyer needs money for only a short time, figuring to complete the job in 2 or 3 months and then sell or refinance it, the investor might consider just setting up a charge account with a hardware store, lumberyard, or home center.

It is a good idea to take out an account with one or more of these suppliers anyway, and establishing an installment payment account would be a good idea if the debt is short-term. (The 18 percent finance charge typical at these stores obviously should not be carried for long when cheaper financing can be arranged elsewhere.)

The strategy that has been described here is to obtain the original property with as little money down as possible, take out a property improvement loan or finance the rehabilitation out of available cash, and then either sell the building or refinance it at its value after the rehabilitation.

To see how the whole process works, assume that the investor has been able to purchase a four-flat for $80,000, with the seller (or another investor or any other source) holding a second mortgage for $12,000. The first mortgage, arranged through a conventional lender, amounts to $64,000, so the buyer only has $4000 cash in the property.

The rehabilitation might cost $2000 per unit, or $8000, which the investor obtains through a property improvement loan with no money down. Still he has only $4000 in the property.

After the improvement, the rents go up, the value is appraised at $100,000, and the investor sells the building at that price. He can now pay off the $64,000 mortgage (assuming no prepayment penalty), the $12,000 second mortgage, and the $8000 property improvement loan—a total of $84,000. Costs of the loan and resale might run another $6000, so the investor has actually realized about $10,000 in a few months on the original investment of $4000.

If the investor chooses to hold the property as a rental building after the same rehabilitation, the original lender can be asked to refinance the property on the basis of its new value of $100,000. The lender now provides $80,000, or 80 percent of the $100,000 value. The investor pays off the $64,000 original mortgage and the $8,000 property improvement loan for $72,000. That leaves $8000 to apply toward the downpayment, along with the original $4000, so he must come up with only $8000.

Of course, the investor could also not pay off the $8000 property improvement loan and then would have the whole downpayment toward the new mortgage, with only $4000 cash actually involved in the ownership of a $100,000 property. The problem in this strategy is that the investor would owe three people—the lender on the first mortgage, the holder of the $12,000 second mortgage, and the lender on the improvement loan. That is a hefty load to carry, but, for a person making a good, steady income, it is a way to leverage everything, take maximum tax advantage of the investment, and await the proper moment to sell for top profit.

The most frequent financing program for a rehabilitation involves convincing a lender of the credibility of the project and having that lender as a partner throughout. This is accomplished by initially proving to the lender that you know what you are doing, have not underestimated how much it will cost or how long it will take, and have plans that indicate exactly how the ugly duckling will become a swan.

Lenders do not like to talk about high-flown ideas for a rehab project. They like to look at plans from a reputable architect or contractor if the rehabilitation is more than just paint-up and fix-up. Therefore, it will be necessary to find such people, get their advice, then have them draw up solid plans for accomplishing your goals.

Stated below are typical fears of a savings and loan association executive when asked about rehabilitation loans. These are fears that have to be arrested by the investor when approaching the lender with a presentation of plans for a building:

> People who aren't sophisticated about rehabbing buildings run out of money because they don't figure the costs right. All of a sudden the lender becomes a reluctant partner and has to come up with more money. That jeopardizes our position because it gives a lower ratio of the loan to the value of the property.
>
> These investors should know a lot about themselves—whether they really will stick to it when the work becomes tiring and they have other things to do.
>
> One thing investors seem to misunderstand is that when they just cure maintenance problems that the previous owner has deferred, they aren't really adding much, if anything, to the value of the property. They're just doing what is necessary to keep the building functioning, not making it more desirable so a renter will pay more to live there.

All of these fears are legitimate and should be concerns of the investor as well as the lender. Consider the solutions one at a time:

Figuring the costs is a difficult matter. However, if your original inspection of the building was done by a competent contractor, architect, or other knowledgeable person, you should be able to persuade the bank that your estimates are not off the top of the head. That you are responsible is demonstrated by the kind of expert advice you have sought.

It is important, though, that the lender recognize and respect your expert. Therefore, ask the person who has estimated your costs of rehabilitation to indicate lenders involved with previous rehabilitation projects. Estimates by a contractor or architect who is known to one or several lending institutions are likely to be acceptable. Also, ask the lender before hiring such a person. It is too late when you have paid someone to cost out a rehabilitation if that person has been consistently low, and the lender knows it.

If the project is not of such magnitude that you need estimates of costs—if your only requirement to rehab a building are landscaping, painting, cleanup, recarpeting, floor sanding, or any other minor aspects of rehabilitation—then estimates from a home center, paint store, plant nursery, carpet store, or other source of materials and supplies would be acceptable to the lender. In these cases, it is assumed that you will do the work yourself or bear any labor costs separately.

It is when you get into construction—changing room sizes, putting in new baths or kitchens, finishing unfinished areas, rewiring, combining, or separating units—that the lender expects you to know exactly what you are doing and how much it will cost.

Lenders also like to see a sense of responsibility on the part of the rehab investor. "If a person has done a successful project before, we are likely to finance the next one," said one lender. "But, if they haven't, we want to see some evidence that they are responsible in other ways."

One way would be to have a savings account to which you regularly add. Another is to hold a job for some time. Anything else that can show a responsible attitude should be included in the investor's personal credit history, which also should accompany the application for a loan.

Assume, though, that the investor has not had time to develop a good credit record or that the job history shows a number of changes. Then it is better to go the other routes described in this chapter—to buy the property and improve it as funds become available and avoid the necessity to obtain an "end" loan before the property is rehabbed.

After it is rehabbed, the lender becomes a believer. After all, the evidence is there in plain sight that the investor had the staying power to go through with the rehabilitation. The next time the investor wants to undertake such a project, what already has been accomplished can be seen, and the lender will take that achievement into full account and usually grant the loan.

The first-time rehabber can also impress the lender by personal references, job improvement (even if there are many jobs involved), low level of debt, knowledge of construction (if any), previous acumen in selecting real estate (a home that seems to be a good investment), or even academic accomplishments.

The point being emphasized here is that first-time investors have to do more to argue their case with the lender when they are asking for a big loan on a somewhat dubious investment. ("Dubious investment" to some lenders is anything that is not located in a stable, medium-to-high income area).

That is, the investors must come across as knowing what the property's potential might be, having the know-how or professional help to realize that potential, and having realistic ideas of the cost and time involved. They must also make a personal impression as responsible and capable of taking on a risky situation and seeing it through. Anything they can provide to the lender that helps confirm those impressions should be part of the presentation.

The last fear of the lender, that the investor simply does not understand what makes a building more valuable, has been discussed previously. The point of emphasis in the presentation should be those items of rehabilitation that are visible and that will persuade a tenant that the unit is worth more rent than before it was upgraded.

So, concede, if necessary, that the building needs electric and plumbing work or a new heating plant. But, also point out that this was one reason it was priced below the market. The difference in value of a building that obviously needed maintenance work and one that did not should have been taken into account in the price of the property. Why should the lender penalize the building again by not agreeing that, when these maintenance factors were taken care of, the building would reach the same value level as buildings where the maintenance had not been deferred?

Thus, a building that the owner was willing to sell for $80,000 because it was obvious that the heating system needed replacement, might have been worth $90,000 without that flaw. Replacement of the heating system was a known factor in the price, and the lender should be willing to recognize that this was the reason the property sold for less than what it would have commanded in the market if the heating plant had been in good repair.

Still, the things an investor plans that do not relate to deferred maintenance impress the lender most. For example, the lender will think you are really doing something:

- If baths and kitchens are to be upgraded

- If two units are to be made out of one
- If small bedrooms are to be combined to add a fine master bedroom
- If an attic or basement is to be finished
- If the floors are to be recarpeted or restored to original quality
- If paneling is to be added where it will be most appreciated
- If landscaping is to be made more attractive

These are the visible items that can mean higher rents and higher value for the property, so the lenders like to see plans that include such changes.

Everything that will be done to raise rents and increase the value of a building should be stated in writing in the presentation to the lender for the permanent financing—the financing of the after-rehab building.

"It takes longer to arrange loans for these rehab properties because many borrowers walk into the lender's office with nothing more than vague ideas for renovation," says Norman Strunk, executive vice president for the United States League of Savings Association. "They haven't translated these ideas into detailed plans and specifications, along with estimated costs of materials and labor. Doing so takes time, but it is necessary before the whole cost picture can be seen."

With plans, personal credit record, and projected rent schedule in good form, the investor goes to one or several lenders to see what terms can be arranged. The lender who has been active in the neighborhood is the first target. Any other lenders who service the area and want to see it improve for their own benefit should also be contacted. Ask for an appointment with a mortgage loan officer who specializes in rehabilitation loans.

Four things are necessary to negotiate with the mortgage officer at this point:

1. The interest rate
2. The method of buying the building and paying for construction
3. The amount of the end loan after rehabilitation
4. The length of the end loan

Interest rates are set by the market and by how much the investor can afford to offer as downpayment. A first-time investor might not get the good deal that a regular customer would. Instead of paying the 10 percent market rate, a first-time investor might be offered a 10.25 percent rate. That is why shopping around often pays off. One association might have plenty of money to lend and a need to get it placed, while another can afford to deal only with regular customers or people who will pay an extra quarter point or more.

A higher downpayment gives the lender more confidence in the borrower and in the likelihood that the project will be completed. If you can put down 30 instead of 20 percent, you will usually be able to negotiate some break on the interest rate, maybe a quarter point less than the market.

Most lenders who are into rehabilitation like to give you all the money needed to buy the building, but schedule payments on the construction—maybe 30 percent at the start, then another 20 percent of the cost after 30 days of work, and so on until the rehabilitation is finished. That keeps the lender's commitment even with the pace of construction, so if something happens and construction stops, the lender will not be out the whole amount to be advanced.

Some lenders even pay the contractors directly as the construction continues and invoices are rendered for completed work. Contractors are willing to accept this system, because they know the money has been committed and will be released when they have done the job.

But, the system should be established before the job gets underway and be part of the lender's original commitment, as will be discussed later.

So should the amount of the permanent loan. The lender will send an appraiser to look at the property, with instructions to look at the building in its present condition, as well as to project what it would be like after it is rehabilitated according to the investor's plan.

The appraiser will use data from other buildings that have been improved or that are equal to what the rehabbed building will be, in order to estimate what the value will be after the rehabilitation. Especially taken into account will be the new and higher rents that a rehab job would produce. Then, the appraiser gives the lender's underwriting officer (the person who recommends to the institution's loan committee how much mortgage commitment would be justified by the value and other factors) a before-and-after estimate of value.

Assume, for example, that the appraiser says a four-unit building is worth $58,000 in its present state, based on comparable sales and rents of $200 a month for each of the four units. But, if improved so it would compete with buildings that charge $250 a month, the property at the same ratio of six times gross income would be worth $72,000. This is a simplified way of indicating how an appraiser might handle this assignment, but it is often a valid one.

The underwriter might say, we shall loan 80 percent of $72,000 when the project is completed, or $57,600. The lender will then offer to provide an 80 percent mortgage on the building as it stands—80 percent of $58,000, or $46,400—and make available the cash needed for the rehabilitation up to

$57,600. Thus, the investor will have a maximum of $11,200 to put into rehabilitation costs.

After the work is done and paid for, a new mortgage is written by the same lender for 80 percent of the $72,000 after-rehab value.

While it is better to deal with one lender instead of several, the end loan commitment in writing from a banking institution can help the investor go in other directions, if better deals can be arranged that way.

For example, if the property can be purchased for only $50,000 instead of $58,000, the investor has some extra money to use. The seller might be persuaded to take a note due in 6 to 9 months at attractive interest on a contract basis with nothing down. Or, a private investor who knows you have a loan based on a $72,000 value of the property might be persuaded to advance the downpayment or the construction money on a short-term basis.

You might also go on to another institution where property improvement loans are less expensive than at the institution that has made the permanent loan commitment. The piece of paper that indicates the willingness of a lender to finance 80 percent of a $72,000 after-rehab value can provide a lot of leverage with which to maneuver.

But, most often, the investor handles everything through one institution—the original property purchase, the construction loan for rehabilitation, and the final loan. It can save closing costs and other expenses that might be part of a juggling of loans among two or more institutions or individuals.

Finally, the rehab investor wants the longest terms for repayment of the mortgage that a lender will provide, for one good reason—a long-term repayment period reduces the amount of the monthly costs. It is the investor's goal to let tenants pay as much as possible of the finance costs through their rents. If the tenants pay all monthly costs and more, the investor gets cash plus the benefits of interest deductions (plus depreciation).

Obviously, also, interest deductions are higher on a 30- than on a 20-year loan. That is because a higher percentage of the monthly payment to the lending institution consists of interest. The rehab investor is not interested in building up equity with a long-term loan. He wants to produce a profitable building, watch it appreciate in value, then sell or trade it. Therefore, a 30-year loan with payments in the first 5 years that are mostly interest and little principal is much better than a 20-year loan that builds principal but offers lower interest deductions.

So long, that is, as the investor sells or trades the building in 5 years or less. If the investor is in for the long term, for 10 or 20 years as the owner of the same building, the strategy makes less sense. (It is the position of this book that the investor should not stay locked into the same property for more than 7 years, for good reasons that will be explained later.)

As an illustration, a building purchased at 10 percent with a 30-year mortgage would be paid back at $8.78 a month for each $1000 of the mortgage. Thus, a $50,000 loan would require monthly principal and interest costs of fifty times $8.78, or $439. On an annual basis, that would amount to $439 times twelve, or $5268. But, of that $5268, all but about $275 would be interest. If the taxpayer were in the 30 percent tax bracket, the approximately $5000 in interest payments would shelter $1500 of income in the first year.

Now, look at the same situation if the mortgage were for 20 years on the same $50,000 building. Payments then would amount to $9.66 a month per $1000, $483 a month on a $50,000 building, or $5,796 a year. First of all, the investor would be paying out $528 more per year to meet mortgage payments with a 20- instead of a 30-year loan. Second, the interest portion of those payments would be slightly less, and the tax deduction about the same for a taxpayer in the 30 percent bracket. The difference would be that the 20-year loan would accumulate $833 in principal in the first year, compared to only $275 in the 30-year loan.

However, for an investor it is more important to save the extra $528 in payouts for the first few years than to accumulate $558 more in equity ($833 principal on a 20-year loan minus $275 on a 30-year loan). The reason for that is that the investor intends to sell the property at its appreciated value within a few years. The accumulation of equity is not as important to the investor as minimizing costs while holding the property. That saving of $528 in mortgage costs means more to the short-term investor than a few dollars more in principal when the property is sold. The return on investment property should be in the big dollars of appreciation, not in the little gains from accumulated equity. The less an investor has to pay into the process of realizing the dollars, the more leverage there is and the greater the return.

PAYING BACK THE MORTGAGE LOAN

Amortizing a mortgage loan means paying the debt back through installments until it is fully repaid. On most mortgages the repayments are made in equal monthly amounts. For example, on a 25-year loan term at a 9-percent interest rate, the monthly payment would be $8.40 for each $1000 of debt. Over the same 25-year period, at a 10-percent interest rate, the monthly payments would be $9.09 per $1000.

Though the total amount paid each month is equal throughout the term of the loan, the portions of that payment applied to principal and to interest change each month. In the early years of a loan the interest payment is higher because it is figured on the outstanding balance of the amount loaned. As the

HOW DO YOU FINANCE IT? 83

total of the remaining principal declines over the years, the amount applied to interest also declines, and the amount applied to the principal rises.

Thus, in the first year of a 25-year loan at 10 percent interest, $99.56 will be charged in interest for each $1000 borrowed, while the principal will be reduced by only $9.52 per $1000 of debt. At the 10-year mark, interest would amount to $85.78, and principal to $21.09 per $1000 borrowed. Finally, in the

Interest Rate	Monthly Payment (per $1000 borrowed)		
	20-year loan	25-year loan	30-year loan
6	$7.17	$6.45	$6.00
6.25	7.31	6.60	6.16
6.5	7.46	6.75	6.33
6.75	7.61	6.91	6.49
7	7.76	7.07	6.65
7.25	6.82 7.91	7.23	6.82
7.5	6.99 8.06	7.39	6.99
7.75	7.16 8.21	7.56	7.16
8	7.34 8.37	7.72	7.34
8.25	7.51 8.52	7.88	7.51
8.5	7.69 8.68	8.05	7.69
8.75	7.87 8.84	8.22	7.87
9	8.05 9.00	8.40	8.05
9.25	8.23 9.16	8.56	8.23
9.5	8.41 9.32	8.74	8.41
9.75	8.59 9.49	8.91	8.59
10	8.78 9.66	9.09	8.78
10.25	9.82	9.27	8.97
10.5	9.99	9.45	9.15
10.75	10.16	9.63	9.34
11	10.33	9.81	9.53
11.25	10.50	9.90	9.72
11.5	10.67	10.17	9.91
11.75	10.84	10.35	10.10
12	11.02	10.54	10.29
12.25	11.19	10.72	10.48
12.5	11.37	10.91	10.68
12.75	11.54	11.10	10.87
13	11.72	11.28	11.07
13.25			
13.5	12.08	11.66	11.46
13.75			
14	12.44	12.04	11.85
14.5	12.80	12.43	12.25
15	13.17	12.81	12.65

last year of the loan, only $5.29 would go to interest and $99.68 would apply to principal.

The table on page 83 indicates how much must be repaid each month for every $1000 borrowed at rates from 6 to 15 percent. (For a year-by-year breakdown of the amount applied to interest versus the amount used to reduce the principal, see standard amortization tables available from banks, libraries, or book stores.)

In fact—and in summary—this chapter on financing has heavily emphasized the necessity to think in terms of minimizing the number of dollars committed by the investor in favor of whatever responsible means are available to use someone else's money.

The name of this game is *not speculation*. It is *leverage*. Almost every investor in every type of investment looks for the opportunity to leverage—to let another party supply the bulk of the money in return for the entrepreneur's willingness to undertake the hard work necessary to make an enterprise succeed. The investor asks for financial support in exchange for his personal commitment in time and energy to turn a profit.

The advice offered in this chapter can be summarized as follows:

- Explore every alternative to reduce your personal dollar commitment, including partnerships with relatives or friends, government programs, contract sales, short-term notes, deals with the seller, and arrangements with the broker or the broker's contacts.
- Especially consider how the seller can be motivated to assist you by an arrangement that can be mutually beneficial.
- Give the lender whatever is necessary to make him secure in offering you a loan. Provide market data for the area (what rents other units command that are similar to those you will offer after rehabilitation), plans and specifications that show what will be done, cost estimates from reliable sources, and any credit or personal information that would influence a loan officer favorably.
- Consider the alternative ways to handle the rehabilitation after the building has been purchased, including doing the work as funds and vacancies become available; dealing with the same lender through the purchase of the building, rehabilitation loan, and long-term financing; or managing the rehabilitation through a home improvement loan or other secondary source with plans for immediate resale after the rehab program is completed.
- Survey the market to improve the interest rate, the amount of the permanent loan after rehabilitation, and the term (length) of the permanent financing.

The way a rehab investment is financed may be critical to whether it is profitable and how profitable it will be. It is imperative to get the best deal possible in terms of the downpayment, interest rate, and term of a loan in order to come out with the top profit that a rehab project affords.

If a financial institution is involved, it is also important to any further rehab investment that an initial effort by a rehab investor indicate a responsible and professional approach. Often, an institution impressed by an investor's first successful venture will become the financial angel for the next project and many more after that. Try to give your sources of financing good reason to believe in you, and the first rehab profit will not be the last.

6 | FINDING LABOR FOR THE JOB

DOING IT YOURSELF

After the building is selected, purchased, and financed, the question becomes: Who is going to do the work?

The cheapest labor is free labor, the investor's own hands and those of his family and friends who might help without remuneration. The only way this labor can get expensive is when it is done poorly or incorrectly. Then it must be done again at cost of materials and perhaps professional labor, which might first be required to correct the mistakes of the amateurs before getting on with the job itself.

The do-it-yourself rehabber also runs into limitations on his own skills that restrict the amount of work that can be done. *Unless,* that is, the investor learns how to do more than his present skills would permit. Books and magazines are available by the hundreds to show do-it-yourselfers how to undertake jobs they have not done before. Usually, these publications tell the amateur what tools are needed, how to operate them, what to do step-by-step, and everything else that one needs to know to perform that task.

Many rehab investors have used publications available in any good bookstore, plus the assistance of the local hardware store, to do jobs they never felt qualified to do before, including plumbing and wiring work.

The hardware store can be an invaluable aid to a rehabber. As will be pointed out in the section, "Using Your Hardware Store," someone in these stores has knowledge that you can use. This is good expertise to tap because it does not cost anything, and usually the hardware expert knows as much as a contractor about the right use of materials and the proper way to do a job.

The important point about using your own and other free labor is that the job should end up looking as good—or almost as good—as if it had been done by a professional. The key is to take your time, use the right materials, seek advice if things appear to be going awry, and stick with it.

The last point, *stick with it,* deserves emphasis. The problem many do-it-yourself rehabbers have is that a job is started and then abandoned in favor of other, more interesting pursuits. You have to look at yourself objectively. Are you likely to start a job, then procrastinate or be distracted by other interests? If so, the work should be done for you, either by hiring subcontractors or a contractor to take over the whole job.

Because rehab investments prove most profitable if the investor contributes as much as possible of his own labor (or that of family and friends), the use of that kind of labor should be abandoned entirely only if the investor really has no skills or any desire to do menial labor.

It is menial labor, after all, that rehabilitation is all about. One may take pride in the completion of a fine paint job, but it is hard work to wield the rollers and brushes to get to that point (though it is work that some enjoy). Furthermore, there is not even aesthetic pleasure in a wiring or plumbing job that is well-done.

The way most do-it-yourself rehabbers work is to obtain skilled labor for jobs such as wiring and plumbing and then try to do everything else at no labor cost.

Skilled labor does not necessarily mean a subcontractor of the type listed in the yellow pages of the telephone directory. It could be someone you know who is capable of doing a handy job as competently as a professional. It might be the engineer or janitor in the building on the block or nearby who can be induced to drop by for a few hours a week to do for you what he does daily in another building.

One Milwaukee rehab investor who has been successful in turning a quick profit on buildings has done so by collecting a group of coinvestors of an unusual type. They are people with "talented hands," he says. They can do almost any job and do it quickly and professionally. Often, they are full-time, live-in engineers in apartment buildings who are willing to give up their spare hours and days off to participate in a good investment opportunity.

The opportunity is so good because the investor gives them half the profit when the building is sold immediately after it is rehabbed. He has a formal contract with the individuals with the "talented hands," in which they split the profit down the middle. The investor obtains the property with a short-term note, usually 6 months in duration, then turns it over to his skilled partner to transform into a first-rate property, and puts it back on the market in its rehabbed state.

The workmanship is so good that the property gleams after its rehabilitation, and the resale comes quickly enough so the note can be paid off and the profits divided within 6 months after the building was purchased. The investor's cost for interest on the note and for the purchase of materials are deducted from the profit on resale before the proceeds are divided between the partners.

Another investor with a good strategy toward rehabilitation has the good fortune to have a friend of the family who is skilled in almost every phase of carpentry, electric work, and plumbing. He is paid for using these skills, but not nearly as much as the union labor rate.

This investor buys a house (in a good neighborhood) that seems to have little charm. It is priced below the level of other homes in the area because it has no desirable features. With the help of his skilled friend, the investor analyzes the house first to see what can be done to provide a new focus or give it a changed look.

The investor buys the house and moves into it, so it will not be sitting empty with neither income nor savings on rent for the investor. He expects to live in each home for at least a year, working on various features in his spare time and calling on the skilled friend when more difficult tasks are to be performed.

In one home they tackled, a long cold basement was finished with paneling, a built-in wet bar, a wall system divider to provide playroom space on one side, and other handsome appointments. The basement became the focal point of the house and proved to be its most popular feature on resale—a feature that added substantially to the value of the home.

It is important to try to find someone who has skills, but is not in a trade full-time, not only because the price might be better, but because tradespeople might simply be difficult to find and even more difficult to schedule. Especially in areas where a substantial amount of rehab work is occurring, tradespeople may be booked for weeks in advance. Or, they are tied up by their steady customers, the general contractors.

One investor got around this problem by moving into a rehab property for a stay of at least 1 and usually up to 2 years. The investor visited tradespeople who would be needed, and advised them of the work to be done, adding, "Do it when you have a slack period; I'm in no hurry."

Eventually, even the busiest tradesperson has a slack period, and sometime it might even be the next day. By having the flexibility to do the work at the tradespeople's convenience, the investor always got the work done—maybe in 3 days, maybe in 3 months.

Another couple used skilled tradespeople every step of the way on their initial rehab project. But, they decided they would try not to be at the mercy of the tradespeople as to scheduling work again. Therefore, they watched the work in progress and asked questions. They were surprised at how willingly the tradespeople answered their questions and demonstrated how to do the job. On the next rehab project they tried, the couple felt confident enough, with help and advice from their hardware merchant, to do the work they had subcontracted to have done previously.

The goal of the investor should be to work toward getting the job done with a minimum of expensive labor. There is little flexibility in the purchase of materials, but there is much to be saved in the purchase of labor, usually 75 percent or more of the total cost.

USING YOUR HARDWARE STORE

The rehab investor's best friend, according to many who have completed these projects successfully, is the hardware store salesperson or manager, who consistently offers good information and advice through the course of the work.

This counsel is free, too. At least, it is free to the extent that if you become a customer for the materials needed in a rehab project, most hardware-store and home-center workers will lend their time and expertise to helping you do the job right. They also will recommend tradespeople to do the work for which you are not qualified.

Some of the hardware stores that specialize in home improvement materials will even send employees out to look at what you plan to do. They will tell you what you need in the way of materials, how long it is likely to take, and roughly what it will cost.

Because they are dealing with professionals in construction as well as amateurs, they also will be helpful in choosing a reputable and competent subcontractor or contractor when such assistance is required.

Frank Scherer operates a hardware store that is especially popular with rehabbers in a hotbed of rehabilitation around DePaul University on Chicago's north side. He points out:

> We always have two or three people on the floor who can give information to do-it-yourselfers and even to skilled laborers who might need their memories refreshed about something. What we don't know, we look up because we don't get into the position of guessing.

Good hardware merchants can tell by talking to a rehabber how familiar the person is with the job to be performed. They often will take special pains with the beginner, demonstrating how a replacement part goes in or how an attachment should be made. It is good business to do so because hardware store customers develop strong loyalties.

According to experienced rehabbers, these are the characteristics of a good hardware store or home center for the do-it-yourself investor in rehabilitation:

- A broad variety of merchandise of each type so that a selection can

FINDING LABOR FOR THE JOB | 91

be made on the basis of size, strength, type, price, and other factors

- Special services, such as a glass replacement shop to which the rehabber can bring a whole door and have the glass replaced on the premises
- A loose assortment of nails, screws, and other essentials so that it is not necessary to buy a package of ten when only two or three are needed
- A good selection of literature on how to do certain types of jobs, with step-by-step instructions
- Modified self-service that permits easy browsing, but that keeps store employees available for help and advice
- Employees who know the building code

Rehabbers suggest that shoppers make a list for the hardware store as they would for the grocery. Then, check out bargain counters for future needs. When a part is to be replaced, bring it along to match it exactly the first time.

ACTING AS YOUR OWN GENERAL CONTRACTOR

Many rehabbers appoint themselves as the general contractors, responsible for buying most materials and choosing and scheduling the work of subcontractors. They do not have the time or inclination to do any of the work themselves. Such a plan is most workable when subcontractors are readily available. It is more difficult and sometimes impossible if the investor needs to get the work done in a hurry and the subcontractors simply cannot get to the job anytime soon.

But, assuming that tradespeople can be found, the question arises as to whether they are qualified and honest. Your lender probably will know. Financial institutions that provide rehab loans make it a point to know who is responsible when a project ran into trouble. If the subcontractors were at fault, the lender will know who they were.

- In a case where you do not know anything about a company, ask for references. If the company is reputable, it will supply references without argument.
- Try to obtain an estimate of the time involved on a job if you go the route of acting as your own general contractor.
- One subcontractor may charge a lower rate, but take much longer to do the work. When the subs are on the job, check on them

occasionally to be sure you are getting performance for the hours you are being charged.

In most cases, there really is no contract with a subcontractor. An estimate is given, the investor says go ahead, and the work is scheduled. An hourly rate is typical for carpentry, plumbing, and electric work. Drywall may be charged by the square foot, and floor sanding and carpet laying by the job.

Whatever the basis for payment, the investor should be satisfied with the job before full payment is rendered. Inspect the work carefully and point out any flaws that should be corrected. If the tradesperson knows there will not be full payment until the job is done right, they will be corrected.

Certainly, if the job requires a building permit, full payment should not be made until the local building inspector has approved it. Subcontractors will try to claim full payment when they think the job is over. But, it really is not over until you and the building inspector are satisfied.

The investor who chooses to act as his own general contractor becomes manager of the project, rather than a direct labor participant. That is important to remember, because if the work is not managed properly, it may take longer than anticipated and probably will be more expensive.

The most common mistake of the first-time general contractor is to schedule tradespeople unrealistically. The electric work is not finished before the carpenter is there. Or, the carpet layers arrive before the painters are through.

Try to pin the subcontractors down as to how long they will take and when they will arrive. Advise them that the work must be completed by a certain date because another phase of the job must start the next day. Then give yourself a few days in between, if possible. It is unlikely that a job can be planned so precisely that as one subcontractor finishes, the next is there to do his part of the work.

USING A GENERAL CONTRACTOR

Acting as your own general contractor saves money in almost every case in which the work proceeds at a respectable pace and with enough attention by the investor to be sure it is quality work. However, many rehabbers would not touch the tricky job of managing all of this activity themselves. If there is more than one or two tradespeople to deal with, they employ a general contractor to handle the whole project.

With the general contractor, you do have a contract. And, a devious instrument it can be if the investor does not examine it closely. Try to think of every contingency while reading the contract. What happens if the work is not satisfactory? What happens if it does not meet the building code? What happens in the event of a cost overrun? What if the contractor runs into unexpected problems in the course of construction? What if the work is late so that tenants scheduled to occupy the property cannot move in?

Unless these matters are covered in the contract, the general contractor will simply point out that there is nothing in writing on that subject—"Sorry." Ask the above questions and others that occur to you in reading the contract. Change the language to put into writing what happens in these cases, if necessary.

Some rehabbers who prefer to turn the bulk of the work over to a general contractor still like to do at least a part of the job themselves. Therefore, a contract should specify the limits of the job as well as its dimensions. The general contractor might otherwise handle everything, and the investor might end up paying skilled labor to do relatively unskilled work.

Sources of information about qualified general contractors include financial institutions who have financed previous work by the contractors and individual tradespeople. Carpenters, electricians, plumbers, and mechanical workers have been employed by several contractors and know the competent ones.

It is also a good idea to call several references that the reputable contractor should be willing to supply. Ask how the job went, whether it was completed on time, what problems were encountered, and whether the job has turned out to be satisfactory over the long run.

A contractor accomplishes many things for the investor that he otherwise would have to do personally. For example, the contractor obtains the building permit for the job. The contractor also should guarantee in writing that there is adequate property damage insurance and liability insurance in case a worker is injured or a neighbor's property is damaged in the course of your construction job.

(If you act as your own general contractor, check your homeowners' insurer to be certain that coverage is sufficient for the rehab work and be sure subcontractors guarantee that they accept insurance liability for their own workers.)

It is important that you also obtain from the general contractor a waiver of lien from subcontractors and materials suppliers. You will have to ask for this important document because it usually is not volunteered. It protects you in case the contractor fails to pay somebody. For example, the contractor might not pay the lumberyard or carpenter. Without a waiver of lien, the lumberyard or carpenter could come after the person who now possesses the materials or who benefited by the work performed.

It is the general contractor's responsibility to buy and pay for materials and subcontracted labor. The investor should be responsible only for paying the general contractor. Moreover, the general contractor should accept in writing all responsibility for worker's compensation insurance or any other insurance necessary for the job.

Once the proper protections are in place, the investor who hires a general contractor can, in most cases, be relieved of concerns that the job will progress rapidly with qualified tradespeople handling the work. Contractors make more money if they can get jobs over with as soon as possible, so they keep the subs moving along in the right order and at the right time. Because they supply most of the work to some tradespeople, general contractors have leverage in commanding their time and skills.

General contractors also want to render satisfaction so the customers will recommend them to others. Many general contractors specialize in rehab projects; therefore they anticipate problems that an amateur or a newcomer to rehab work would not expect or know how to handle.

With proper safeguards, then, the general contractor can do a lot for the rehab investor to be sure a project does not bog down or fail to accomplish what was planned.

Here are Seattle contractor Robert L. Logan's tips about working with general contractors:

> To find out about past performance, check with the Better Business Bureau or the Consumer Information Service that some communities maintain. Or, go to a reputable lumberyard, and ask for recommendations. Check out references. Any reputable contractor welcomes an investigation.
>
> Contractors can help you find the most favorable places to get financing for the job. It is in their best interest to know where the money is coming from.
>
> Contractors can give you good estimates at the beginning as to what materials will be needed and provide accurate estimates of cost as they get further into the job.
>
> Many contractors refuse to get into a bidding war. If they know that you are getting three or four bids and planning to take the lowest, they will not get involved. Shopping several contractors does not accomplish that much because if the specifications are the same, they will come in very close in price. Select one that you have checked out so you have confidence in the contractor's honesty and can expect to get your money's worth.
>
> It's no insult to a contractor to ask for a certificate of insurance. The customer should also obtain a waiver of lien for both labor and materials. The material supplier will provide this waiver, protecting the customer. But it's more paperwork and the contractor won't supply it unless asked to do so.
>
> If you have any questions or apprehensions about a contractor's work while the job is in progress, don't let it grow. Ask about it when the question arises.

FINDING LABOR FOR THE JOB

When you select a contractor and the job is just about to begin, the matter of dollars and stages of work should be in writing. But, it's impossible to put every detail into the contract. Mutual trust is needed. If changes are requested in the course of the work, ask the contractor if they will affect cost. Sometimes, they will result in less cost. Maybe the customer will decide on shelves to divide two rooms instead of a wall. Shelves might be cheaper than a wall. But, ask what effect the change will have on the cost of the job, so there will be no surprise when the final bill is rendered.

The contractor has an obligation to do the job right and tends to use the people who are most competent. In effect, the contractor does most of the selling and promotion for the subcontractors, and so gets a price break from them. However, the contractor is as interested as the customer in making the experience a pleasant one for both.

Try to develop good relationships with the contractors. They'll do extra for you if you treat them as professionals.

The points are well taken, but still the investor should seek to have put in the contract some method of settling issues that may arise during the construction. They can be handled through an arbitration process, which is a common mechanism in many contracts. In the event of a dispute, the Better Business Bureau or some other impartial agency hears both sides and either suggests a compromise or rules for one or the other. It is a lot easier than threatening legal action and raises less animosity.

The advantage to using a general contractor is that the investor with no skills or interest in rehab work can get a high-quality job done in a hurry by competent tradespeople and responsibility is vested in one source who can be expected to guarantee the work and absorb all the headaches.

The disadvantage is the 10 to 15 percent that the contractor puts into the bill as payment for doing the job.

Veteran rehabbers also caution that contractors have a tendency to quit a job too soon and leave out the finishing touches as they hasten on to the next job. Therefore, they advise the rehabber to hold back "tactfully" the last 5 to 10 percent of the payment to the contractor until full satisfaction is achieved.

"They want to be in and out as fast as possible," said one rehabber. "Furthermore, their workers don't like those finishing touches, such as putting on the plates for electrical outlets and testing the switches. So, try to hold back some of your payment until they have really finished the work."

The contractor typically is paid 20 to 30 percent upfront, part of which may be used to purchase necessary materials. Then, a schedule is established between the rehabber and the financial institution as to further payments as the work progresses. The lender wants a schedule of payments on the basis of work completed. Usually, there are three or four payouts made directly to the contractor by the lender.

Good protection to the rehabber is afforded by such a system, so it is not done just for the lender's benefit. For example, if the contractor does not produce, the rehabber can take advantage of a waiver that should be in the contract to terminate the job for nonperformance. Even though there may be some loss in having a new contractor pick up the job there, at least the amount will be minimal compared to full payment.

A second benefit to the rehabber is that interest does not begin to apply until the money is actually borrowed. Only the amounts paid out to date would bear interest until the full payout.

WORKING WITH AN ARCHITECT

One other route to consider is the use of an architect who also acts as general contractor to the extent of selecting materials and recommending or hiring particular tradespeople to do the work. An architect usually has more knowledge of materials and almost as much knowledge of good subcontractors as a general contractor. The architect also will develop plans that should be more imaginative, that could save on costs, and that will be more responsive to an investor's goals.

The use of an architect especially makes sense if the investor does not have a clear concept of what should be done to a property or if there is anything complex about the contemplated improvements. For example, if the changes in the property include the addition of a room or garage, or substantial interior renovation, an architect's services would be important, if not essential.

For one thing, the local building department would expect detailed architectural drawings for such a project. General contractors can supply such drawings, but they also have architects do them in many cases, with the customer paying the architects' fees indirectly.

Selection of an architect should be made through a process similar to the selection of a general contractor or subcontractor: Ask the financial institution, lumberyard, or hardware store owners and other rehabbers. Not all architects are qualified to do rehab work. Some architects specialize in this work, and they can do it more rapidly with better grasp of the rehab goals and with the possibility that they can handle the subcontract work through tradespeople they know from previous jobs.

There are, however, some problems that can arise through the use of an architect. Number one is cost. Architects often have less sense of what a project will cost than general contractors, who are dealing with the market every day. Architects also can get carried away with the design so that it accomplishes more than it needs to as an investment. Good aesthetics are valuable, up to a point, but, when they cost more than they will return in rents or resale value, the added cost becomes an unnecessary expense.

Consider the statement of Chicago investor William White:

> We worked with an architect for a year to get our plans the way we wanted them. The problem was that my wife and I had entirely different ideas of how we wanted to rehab the second floor of the house we bought. I would advise all rehab investors to come to agreement between husband and wife or between partners before going to an architect or general contractor.
>
> Finally, we gave the architect a budget that we secretly were prepared to exceed by one-third. He kept telling us that there was no problem with the costs. But, when the estimates came in, they were 50 percent higher than even the amount we secretly agreed we would accept.
>
> Architects tend to overdesign. They also use materials with which most tradespeople are not familiar. Tradespeople don't like to experiment with new materials.

Architects work either on a fixed-fee or percentage basis, depending on whether they are just hired to handle the design and draw the plan or also get involved in the work on the site by hiring subcontractors. They should make inspections in either case, to be sure the work is done correctly. In negotiating fees with an architect, it is advisable at least to have some general idea what the project will look like when completed. Then, the architect can make a quick calculation of the time that will be needed to develop plans to produce that result and estimate a fee without delay.

The investor who employs an architect should do so:

1. When the work involves combining rooms or adding rooms
2. When extra quality is desired, with the use of finer materials or more imaginative design
3. When something is being added to the house, such as a room or garage
4. When the architect is noted for both good design and for overseeing the work of selected tradespeople to produce top quality

Many investors will do as much as possible by themselves on the first job, then, on subsequent projects, enjoy the luxury of an architect or general contractor.

7 | BUILDING PERMITS AND INSPECTIONS

Building permits are almost always required when alterations, additions, new construction, repairs of a substantial nature, or razing are being undertaken (Figure 7–1). When a permit is issued, it means that a building inspector will check out the work to assure that it meets local zoning and building codes.

Examples of the kinds of projects for which you will need a building permit in most communities include:

- Replacing siding
- Building a new porch (in some areas, also repairing a porch)
- Replacing existing masonry
- Replacing the roof
- Finishing off rooms in the attic or basement
- Enclosing and heating porches
- Adding a garage or breezeway
- Changing from single- to multiple-family dwelling
- Constructing or altering plumbing system
- Installing, replacing, or extending warm-air furnaces
- Shoring, raising, or moving any building
- Erecting chimneys
- Building mechanical or exhaust ventilation system
- Building fences over 5 feet high
- Installing boilers
- Installing driveways
- Installing or altering electric equipment
- Constructing, altering, or adding ventilation
- Adding facilities

Figure 7-1 A building permit is necessary for most construction work in a rehab project.

Permits are usually not required for minor repairs or anything that can be characterized as maintenance. Under maintenance would be included the repair or replacement of most existing components of the building (though not the furnace or roof). Painting and floor sanding would be considered maintenance, not requiring a building permit.

Zoning codes must also be taken into account when the investor plans to increase (and sometimes decrease) the number of units in a building. Often, such a change requires an application to zoning officials for a variance from the present use of the building. The investor will be required to show that the change in the building will not alter the basic character of the neighborhood or impose hardship on residents of nearby buildings.

One of the best plans an investor can have is to increase the number of units in a building, so it is important to know before the purchase of a property for that purpose whether the zoning agency would approve such a plan. It pays to check with the local zoning board first. A zoning officer will acquaint you with the applicable zoning for that area and give you preliminary advice as to whether an increase in units is feasible.

Making a basement into a living unit requires the approval of both building and zoning departments. Most local building ordinances specifically prohibit living units below the surface. Typically, no living unit will be permitted more than 2 feet below grade, and the ceiling height of *any* unit that extends below grade must be at least 8 feet.

For any project of substantial nature, the building department will be more likely to accept plans drawn up by an architect or contractor. An owner's plans also may be accepted if they comply with building codes. A rewiring job or the completion of an unfinished basement would require detailed plans that probably should come from an architect or contractor. So would kitchen or bathroom modernization if plumbing or wiring were involved.

The building and zoning agencies were established to protect the public from shoddy work and disorderly development. Personnel of these agencies usually are sympathetic to people who are trying to upgrade buildings through rehabilitation. So do not be afraid they will scuttle your plans out of bureaucratic nit-picking. More often, they will be helpful in suggesting ways to accomplish a plan more effectively.

The cost is minimal. Figure on about $20 to $30 for the basic building permit and perhaps additional small fees for inspections of the electric, plumbing, or heating work.

Building inspectors maintain that "rehabbers should have nothing to fear from an inspection because they are changing the things that are wrong about the building anyway as they go about their rehabilitation. Our inspection gives them a starting base to do what is needed."

The two most common areas for violation of building codes are electric and plumbing systems. Insufficient electric outlets, wiring that is not of an acceptable gauge, or an inadequate fusing system all could be cause for a citation from the building inspector.

The plumbing might not be properly vented, or a bathroom might need additional equipment to conform to local standards. Some building codes require that every bathroom have a sink, for example.

Any of the experts you employ to inspect the property before you buy should be able to list all code violations without difficulty. The buyer has the additional protection that the standard sales contract says the seller must disclose any notices received from the municipality regarding code violations. Otherwise, if it is found later that a prior notice of violation was not revealed, the sale could be declared null and void.

During the rehabilitation itself, it is important when dealing with a subcontractor or contractor who is going to do the rehab work, that it be established in writing that the work will comply with the building code.

It should also be noted that building departments in some cities insist that a rehabilitation involving electric or plumbing work be handled exclusively by "licensed contractors"—a euphemism for union tradespeople. When building agency personnel make their inspection, they will ask to see proof that a union tradesperson was involved. On most other work besides electric and plumbing, the building inspectors will permit the investor to register as general contractor and do most of the work personally or subcontract out. So, be sure to find out what the customs are with regard to union labor.

Buildings of more than six units usually are inspected every year at a small fee of $10 to $35. Smaller buildings are inspected only when an area is being surveyed every few years or when someone has made a complaint. Anyone can register a complaint in most cities, often without having to be identified to the property owner.

When a simple violation is found, the building department will send a notice to the owner and reinspect the property a short time later to be sure the violation has been taken care of. A more serious violation might require an administrative hearing at a compliance board to report on progress made to rectify the problem. If the owner does not respond to a citation, the building is reinspected, and the case is sent to the corporation counsel for litigation.

Serious violations can result in the building department filing for compliance within 24 to 48 hours. Failure to comply could mean that the building will be emptied of tenants because of the hazard.

(That is the way some investors get rid of unwanted tenants while they rehabilitate a building. It saves them the problem of issuing eviction notices, with the hostility that such action often arouses. When the municipality issues the eviction notices, it takes off much of the heat.)

In every project involving government funds, local building inspectors will look at the property. Sometimes, when minor rehab work is done by a property owner, a building inspection is never made. Some rehabbers like it that way. Others feel that it is good protection for the buildings, the tenants, and their own welfare to go ahead and ask for the inspection.

8 | MAKING COSMETIC IMPROVEMENTS

WORKING AROUND TENANTS

As you get ready to start work, with labor arranged and building permits in hand, a big handicap will be apparent to the investor in a two- to six-flat. At the same time, this apparent handicap can also be an important advantage.

The reference here is to the tenants still occupying the building. They might have months or even years left on their leases, and, just because the building has changed ownership in favor of an investor who wants to rehabilitate it, they have no intentions of moving out.

Nor does the investor necessarily want them to move out. During the terms of their leases, they are helping to make the mortgage payments. Without that income, many investors would be hard-pressed to pay financing costs.

The term of existing leases should be taken into full account before a building is purchased, especially if the investor intends to upgrade the building for quick resale. It can be awkward, if not impossible, to rehab a building where the tenants have leases that protect them from unnecessary entry to their units or provide for rents for some long period of time that are out of line with what the rehabbed building should return.

Ideally, no lease will extend longer than 1 year. An owner is not required to renew a lease, so the tenant can be advised with due notice—usually 30 days—that the apartment will have to be vacated so that it can be renovated.

An interesting strategy to deal with tenants was adopted by a rehab investor who specialized in three-flats. The investor moved into the first available unit and began the process of rehabbing in that apartment and in all the common areas, including the yard. The tenants were well aware that their building was being improved because it was better maintained, the landscaping was upgraded, the common hallways were recarpeted, and workers were busy inside the owner's apartment.

They also knew that as their leases expired, they would be expected to move or pay significantly higher rents. That is precisely what the investor wanted the tenants to realize. As lease expiration neared, the owner offered to make certain modest improvements in their apartments, such as new appliances for the kitchen, but indicated that the rent would increase by at least 20 percent.

The investor did not particularly care whether the tenant stayed or moved out, but benefited either way. With only a token improvement to the apartment, the investor would get a big increase in rent. If the tenant chose to move, then all the necessary work in the apartment to obtain the desired rent could be done. If anything, the investor would rather the tenant stayed and, therefore, tried to make living there more comfortable and take care of minor annoyances that the tenant might have had.

It is important to be sympathetic and considerate of tenants. They might even agree to let their apartment be rehabbed without moving out. Or, they might agree to supply the labor if you supply the materials for improving the property.

Replacing good tenants is expensive and time-consuming. Therefore, you want to try to hold onto them if it is possible to do so without sacrificing the rehab program for the building.

Investors who expect to hold a building for several years plan their rehab program to do each unit as the leases expire. After the first unit is rehabbed, they offer it to other tenants in the building at the higher rent. Often, one of the existing tenants will agree to give up a current lease in order to make the easy move into a better apartment in the same building. Then, that unit can be rehabbed too.

Dealing with the tenants is part of a later chapter on managing the building as a rental property. However, it is important from the beginning to try to secure the support and interest of the tenants already in a building purchased for rehab. They can help or get in the way and cause problems. Be frank as to what you intend to do with the building. If feasible to do so, give them some amenity right away—perhaps a window air conditioner or a new appliance.

Also, handle their maintenance problems as soon as possible to show that the building is going to be run more efficiently from now on. Nobody likes to move, and tenants who are shown that there is good reason to stay put, even at higher rents, often will choose that option.

The number one goal of the investor should be to improve the property only enough to bring in the high rents that will make the building more valuable. *Anything more than that is superfluous and a waste of money.* Thus, many of the improvements that might make the property a thing of beauty and an aid to good living should not be undertaken because they do not add enough to the potential value after rehabilitation.

The least expensive changes are those called "cosmetic" because they simply improve the visual appeal of the building without any heavy investment in the structure or mechanical systems. Some investors buy only buildings that are ugly, but otherwise sound. They are more gifted as decorators than as rehabbers. But, even for the investor who intends to go deeper into improving a building, the cosmetics are important.

EXTERIOR COSMETIC IMPROVEMENTS

One of the best places to start cosmetic improvement is the yard. Think about putting a fence around your property. That simple improvement makes the units more valuable to people who have children or pets.

Though the investor may not care to have children or pets on the property, the fact remains that a large segment of the market for rental property is the young family that cannot afford to buy a home yet. And, young families have children who have pets. If the neighborhood is populated by a good percentage of renters in this age bracket, the investor should consider ways to cater to this market. A fence that provides an element of safety for small children and pets can be a good inducement to rent.

As with all improvements, the fence should be constructed with materials that are easy to maintain. Painting a white picket fence every year to keep the property attractive becomes expensive. "Always stain a wood fence with deep-penetrating stain rather than a paint," advises rehab specialist Jerry Field. "It lasts 5 years and doesn't chip off as paint does."

Field also tried to avoid any fence maintenance that would weaken the foundation of the fence. Thus, for the fence rails, Field uses screws instead of nails. When rails have to be replaced, there is no hammering of nails to get them out and then back in when the new rail is added.

Field's thinking illustrates how much attention rehab investors who intend to hold a property give to the long-term costs. These costs will cut into the return on the property unless considered as the improvements are made.

The purpose of any expenditure on the yard is to tell a prospective or current *tenant* that the building is worth the rent asked because it consists not only of the space between the walls, but also an attractive exterior that might be used for recreation or relaxation. It should tell a prospective *buyer* that the building is attractive and probably well-maintained because that is the image it presents.

The cosmetic improvement that rehab investors often make is a new exterior paint job, an improvement that many investors can handle by simply buying the paint and doing it themselves.

Yet, it is not an easy job for the inexperienced painter. Ladders are almost always required, and ladders are hazardous devices. The exterior surface probably will need to be scraped, sanded, and filled with mortar mix, outdoor spackle, or another compound before any paint can be applied. Areas around window frames usually require extra attention, including caulking of the joints and more detailed scraping and sanding work.

Even a brick building can be washed down or sand blasted and tuckpointed, or touched up outside by a paint job on the window frames that can make a significant contribution to the appearance. And, all types of siding can be painted, usually with less preparation.

A professional house painter might be expensive, but worth it. The do-it-yourself painter produces better results on paint jobs inside the house, where the ladders are less dangerous, the preparation of the surface less complex, and the work less physically demanding.

Painting estimates often vary widely and, if a professional painter is used, it would be well to obtain three estimates. Be sure the estimates include preparation of the surface as well as the application of the paint itself.

The importance of a clean, attractive exterior to a building would be difficult to overestimate. The first impression counts most, both to prospective tenants and to the guests who visit them in their apartments. The tenant wants people who come to visit to be impressed with the facade. A dirty, drab exterior to a building gives tenants little or no pride in where they live. It is not something they can do anything about, as they can within their own apartment units.

Therefore, an owner who makes the exterior of the property attractive encourages the tenants to put extra effort into carrying that look through to their own units—often to the extent of spending their own money to add paneling, wallpaper, and other interior touches.

The investor should look at the exterior of the property with just as much concern as the interior. Sometimes it is the key to adding value to the real estate. Consider shutters at the windows, for example. Look at the front door. Distinctive front doors can change the whole look of a home, and they are not very expensive. Consider the exterior lighting. Perhaps a small, inexpensive lamp beside the door or at the entry would add some character and class to the property.

"Curb appeal" is what real estate brokers say a house or building has if it is attractive to anyone passing it at the curb. It is worth thousands of dollars in resale value when that appeal convinces a potential buyer that the building is the equal or superior to anything else in the neighborhood because it is so handsome and well-maintained from the exterior.

Look at these things that can be done to achieve this objective:

- A fence sets a property apart physically and psychologically. It establishes boundaries of safety and ownership of space for the tenants and distinguishes property from others that seem open to anyone who cares to trespass. This improvement also can add to the marketability of the property.

- An attractive yard indicates that the owner cares about the property. It tells tenants, visitors, and neighborhood residents that this building is well-maintained and a source of pride to residents and owner.
- The exterior look of a building that is freshly painted or has interesting windows and doors conveys the same message as a neat yard to those who see it as visitors or passersby.

If a backyard or sideyard can be improved with a modest investment so that tenants would see that outdoor areas would increase the pleasure of living in the building, funds might be committed to such improvements.

For example, if the market is primarily families with children, such items as a basketball hoop over the garage or a sandbox or play equipment might be an investment that would enable the investor to ask higher rates. If the market is primarily single or older couples, an old-fashioned swing, rustic benches, or even a shuffleboard surface might pay off.

In this type of expenditure, the investor wants to give tenants an extra amenity—use of a backyard or sideyard—without committing to what might be an expensive maintenance or security problem. Equipment provided to make the yards more usable should be chosen on the basis of how much cost and effort will be needed to maintain the amenity and how likely it is to be stolen in that neighborhood.

Anything that can be moved easily is subject to theft in the neighborhoods in which most rehab activity occurs, so it should be an important consideration as to whether equipment added to the yard can be bolted down or made more difficult to take away.

INTERIOR COSMETICS

The investor's effort to improve the cosmetic attractiveness of the property now focuses on the interior, which offers many opportunities for this least expensive type of rehab upgrading.

Again, much of the work to make the inside more attractive can be done by the investor and other cheap or inexpensive labor because it is not demanding of professional skills.

Look first at the entry of the building. How does the building appear to someone who sees the interior for the first time? The first impression should be that the building is clean, nicely appointed as to hallway furnishings, and lighted to good advantage.

If an investor is lucky, the building may just need a thorough cleaning. Consider that possibility first because there are few materials involved in cleaning, compared to the cost of paint, wallpaper, and carpet. The labor of cleaning also will cost substantially less, even if the investor does not want to do the work personally. With just a good washing of the walls and ceilings, waxing of the floors or cleaning of carpets, and better lighting to show off the results, a building might be made entirely presentable (Figure 8–1).

In most buildings, cleanup is part of the job of rehabbing. Owners with marginal profits often stop keeping the building clean as one of the ways to save money. Therefore, unless the walls are scarred, painted or papered in the wrong color or style, or too far gone to be simply washed down, consider the possibility of a thorough cleaning to restore them.

The same holds true for the floor or carpet. Sanding a floor is a popular cosmetic improvement. However, maybe the whole floor does not need sanding. Maybe it just needs thorough cleaning and waxing, and the addition of a couple of attractive rugs. If it is beyond that stage, then maybe instead of restoring it, the better alternative would be to carpet the whole area to cover the floor up. Remember, though, that carpet has a short life in a heavily traveled area—4 to 6 years is common. And, carpeting must be cleaned regularly, especially where winters are heavy and mud is regularly tracked over it.

Lighting is one of the most important aspects of a common entryway. The

Figure 8–1 Cleaning the building provides the fresh look that is desired. This investor gives radiators a brush-cleaning.

walls can look fresh and clean, the floor polished and glistening, and the windows treated attractively with drapes or curtains, but none of it shows to good advantage if the lighting is too weak, too strong, or just inappropriate.

Consider a hallway table, with a table lamp and mirror. The lamp does not have to be either big or expensive. It should give a warm feeling to the entry area. When a prospective tenant enters the building, the clean, well-maintained impression should come across immediately. And, the way the area is lighted—not so bright as to be intimidating or so weak as to be dismal—plays an important part in conveying that impression.

Next, the investor wants to improve the eye-appeal of the individual units that are for rent. The key areas to start with are the kitchen and bathroom. Old-fashioned facilities in the kitchen and bathroom probably cost more in rent dollars to a building owner than anything else.

The stove and refrigerator may need replacement with something more modern—not necessarily something new. Look at the advertisements for used appliances. Some stores and individuals have appliances for sale that still have some of the warranty left. Or, they will guarantee the appliance against breakdowns for 90 days.

It is expensive to buy new appliances and probably does not pay off at resale. But, the investor who permits rundown and outdated kitchens to go without any upgrading is making a mistake (Figure 8–2).

These improvements would not all be classified as "cosmetic" so much as practical: The look of a kitchen with ancient cooking and refrigerating equipment is certain to be disappointing. Therefore, newer appliances must be considered, if necessary, to give this vital area a more modern look (Figure 8–3).

Other cosmetic improvements in the kitchen involve giving it better lighting, clean walls and ceilings, and polished or freshly stained cabinets. Make the kitchen glow and you will accomplish a great deal to obtain and retain tenants.

The bathroom is almost as important as the kitchen. It should have an appealing place to apply makeup and shave. Good mirror and counter space can be added without great expense if the bathroom does not have these amenities.

Think in terms of what your tenant would need to get ready in the morning and try to provide those facilities. A large medicine cabinet would be a must if there is a shortage of storage space. If your tenants are likely to have children, more counter and storage space should be added. These additions can be built for less than buying them, but a visit to the kitchen and bath supply stores might discover just what is needed at a cost that might be quickly recoverable in increased rents.

Wallpaper considered for a bathroom should be applicable under a process

Figure 8–2 This tiny kitchen area could be enhanced and expanded by placing a counter in front, arranging the appliances for maximum efficiency, and adding wall-hung cabinets.

that does not peel with high humidity. Hardware store advisers know what wallpapers work best in bathrooms. Semigloss paint should be used for bathrooms because it can be cleaned easily and should not peel in highly humid conditions.

Tile in the bathroom can be a most attractive feature. But, it is likely to add value only if the investor can do the work without heavy labor cost. However, laminated plastic or fiberglass panels that come in many colors may be a good substitute. It is cheaper, easy to install from 4- to 8-foot sheets, and gives something of the same effect of ceramic tile without the problems of stained grout between the tiles and missing tiles that have to be replaced.

When the bathroom already has ceramic tile, but the tile looks soiled and dingy, the solution might be to paint it with an epoxy paint. Missing tiles are easily replaced by using liquid tile cement; then the whole area is painted over. It will withstand water from the shower without showing any discoloring in the joints. The maintenance should be minimal.

The same type of epoxy paint can be used to paint bathtubs and can give an older tub a fresh look without the cost of replacement. However, this type paint does not last well.

(Changes in the plumbing, wiring, and carpentry in the kitchen and bath will

MAKING COSMETIC IMPROVEMENTS | 111

be covered later because these improvements are not considered cosmetic changes.)

Windows represent another area where cosmetic treatment can be applied with good benefit. The paint around windows tends to chip and crack and give a weatherbeaten appearance that can be corrected by sanding and repainting.

Some window frames are made of wood that would be highly attractive if stripped properly and perhaps stained or even left with the original wood look. However, it is a painstaking job to clean and restore wood around windows, and, in economic return, the work involved usually cannot be justified. Rents will not change that much, if any, and the new tenants may prefer that the woodwork be painted over.

"I'm a believer in staining wood surfaces," says rehab investor Jerry Field. "A good coat of stain, and you might not have to bother with it again for 10 years."

Window treatment in the form of blinds, shades, or drapes might do more to attract and keep tenants at acceptable rents. In common areas, expenditure to make the window coverings attractive (without sacrificing much, if any, light)

Figure 8-3 Modernizing the kitchen, with emphasis on counter and cabinet space, has been recognized as the best rehab improvement to make in terms of its contribution to value appreciation.

can give another touch of class to the entryway or other commonly used areas in the building (Figure 8–4).

Normally, window treatment is provided only to the extent of blinds or shades. The tenant who wants drapes or curtains pays for them. Avoid buying new blinds or shades if possible. See if they cannot be cleaned or repaired and made acceptable for tenants. These items are practical and not really cosmetic except in common areas, so they will not do much to encourage better rent levels.

The stairways also lend themselves to cosmetic improvement. A worn carpet on the stairs or a bannister that looks battered and scraped by furniture moving in and out over the years—both can be improved cosmetically as a way to raise upper-floor rents and give an overall boost to the look of the entryway.

The material of most stairway surfaces is wood. If it is covered by carpet, take a peek under the carpet to see what the wood looks like. Maybe it will respond to sanding and staining, a process that is both cheaper and will look good longer than carpet, if done properly.

Figure 8–4 For the special touch of quality, window treatment might include stained glass, instead of blinds or drapes.

MAKING COSMETIC IMPROVEMENTS | **113**

Figure 8–5 One way to deal with an eyesore ceiling is to cover it up with ceiling panels (see p. 114).

Taste in making cosmetic improvements is the key to returning value for the time and money invested. Colors should be coordinated. Dark areas should be made lighter. Special features of an apartment should be brought out and emphasized.

That requires a knowledge of colors and lighting that some people have and some do not. But, almost everyone knows a person whose good taste is evident in the way they have decorated their own properties. Ask for advice from friends who have shown a sense of style and imagination.

In choosing colors of paint, carpeting, and wallpaper, stay on the conservative side, experienced rehabbers advise. Do not try to create dramatic effects that may go unappreciated by those to whom you would rent or sell.

As an example, off-white paint is never a mistake for walls, though it may need more frequent cleaning or repainting. Almost every furniture color and piece of art looks good against an off-white or solid-white background. Blue or grey or pink walls may not suit the color motif of many prospective renters or buyers. They will know as soon as they see the apartment that they will have to bear the expense of a paint job to coordinate their furniture with the walls.

It is also better if the tenant covers the floor with rugs or carpeting that suit

114 | REHABBING FOR PROFIT

his or her decor than if you must try to select a carpet color that will be most likely to satisfy all tastes. (There are not any ideal carpet colors, though beige works with most color schemes.)

If you do intend to put new carpeting in the apartment, try showing it to prospective tenants first without the carpet and offering to let them help decide on the color according to what works best with their color scheme. Such an offer may be the key to renting to a tenant who might have objected to the color of a carpet already selected and installed.

The benefits of an excellent cosmetic job on a building should not be underestimated. While most older buildings will need the construction work that is identified with rehabilitation, the additional commitment to making the property look clean and attractive inside and out can make an even greater difference in the rents that can be charged (Figure 8–5).

So, both in analyzing the building before it is purchased and taking the first step in rehabilitation, identify the simple but important cosmetic improvements that can be made at little expense and with a minimum of skilled labor.

Figure 8–5 continued.

9 | REHAB INVOLVING CONSTRUCTION

ADJUSTING TO YOUR MARKET

After cosmetic considerations have been taken into account, the rehab investor looks for changes in the structure of the property that would add value.

Again, analyze your market in terms of what the building has to offer. See what type people are renting similar apartments in the area and assume that your building will appeal most to that element too. Here are several groups that might be interested in rental property that has been rehabbed, plus the items they especially like to obtain for their rent dollar.

The Couple, No Children, One member Working, One at Home During the Day

1. A well-equipped and modern kitchen because they usually eat three meals at home, including one substantial meal
2. A den or some other area for watching television, reading, or listening to records, which ideally also could be used as a guest room by providing a convertible sofa
3. An area for entertaining friends, usually a living- and dining-room combination
4. An exterior area, such as a patio or a space of sun and shade, that could be furnished to serve as a common outdoor meeting place for those who do not work during the day

The Couple, Both Working, No Children

1. A convenient kitchen with a dishwasher

2. A den that could be used as a guest room
3. Two bathrooms, if feasible; if not, one efficient and modern bathroom
4. A washer and dryer on the property

The Couple with Small Children, One Working, One at Home

1. A modern and well-equipped kitchen, preferably with a dishwasher
2. Air-conditioning in most climates, at least for the bedroom
3. Two or more bedrooms, depending on family sizes in the area
4. Two bathrooms, preferably both with tubs as well as showers
5. A washer and dryer on the property
6. Exterior space that could offer playground or baby-watching facilities to assist the at-home parent

The Couple with School-age Children, Both Working

1. A convenient kitchen with dishwasher
2. Two bathrooms
3. At least two bedrooms
4. A washer and dryer on the property
5. An entertainment area in the basement or yard to interest children

The Single Working Woman or Man

1. A convenient kitchen
2. An area for television viewing, reading, or listening to records
3. A place to eat in the kitchen
4. Air-conditioning in the bedroom

The Older Couple, No Children, One Working, One at Home

1. A modern and well-equipped kitchen
2. Air-conditioning, at least for the master bedroom
3. A washer and dryer on the property
4. A lot of closet and storage space
5. A formal or semi-formal living-room/dining area
6. An exterior area providing common relaxing and meeting space for the members who do not work during the day

The Retired Couple, No Children, Both Living at Home

1. A modern, well-equipped kitchen
2. Air-conditioning in most climates, at least for the master bedroom
3. A washer and dryer on the property
4. A lot of closet and storage space
5. An exterior area providing common relaxing and meeting space for all tenants
6. An area for television viewing, reading, or listening to records

By studying the neighborhood or the previous tenancy of the building, the investor can easily determine which of the above groups will be most likely to rent in the building. Then, the costly improvements—more than the cosmetics changes previously discussed—can be geared to the real needs of that market (Figure 9–1). To spend money that is not directed at the actual market for an apartment risks the likelihood that it will not be recovered in rents. Consider, then, what improvements will most induce the above markets to pay the after-rehab rents.

MODERNIZING THE KITCHEN

The kitchen is the key factor in appealing to almost all of these markets. Study the kitchen to see what it requires to appeal to the particular market the building is likely to serve. Maybe it is just a matter of building additional shelves and drawers or installing a dishwasher. That is enough to satisfy most couples who work full-time, as long as the stove and refrigerator are adequate. However, an expansion of the kitchen, the addition of electric outlets for more

Figure 9-1 For a market of couples with accumulated possessions, a full wall of storage might be a selling feature for an apartment.

appliances, and the provision for more storage space may be necessary if the market consists of families with children or older couples.

Kitchen layout is a service of some contractors who specialize in modernizing kitchens. They will tell you what you need, give you an estimate of the cost, and handle the subcontracting of plumbing, electric, and carpentry work.

A rehab investor can spend $12,000 or more in the kitchen by going all out with tile, cabinets, double sinks, and fancy appliances. Such an investment is almost never recoverable in a rehab project. At most, the rehabber should think in terms of a $3000 to $4000 price for expenditures in the kitchen.

The dishwasher, while highly valued by some groups of tenants, can cost more than it will return in rents if complicated plumbing connections are required. Normally, not much plumbing work is needed. The dishwasher that is close to the hot-water line that feeds to the sink can be installed by the simple connection of a separate pipe and the addition of a hose connection to the drain line of the sink.

Some carpentry work also will be required if the unit is built into the counter and cabinet system. An appliance dealer will tell you what it would cost to install a dishwasher and what plumbing and carpentry work would be needed. Stores that sell appliances do not usually handle any complicated plumbing or carpentry work, but, if the installation is a simple one, the cost will be minimal to do the job.

Without a dishwasher, a double-bowl sink probably will be required to attract tenants. Therefore, consideration of whether to buy a dishwasher should take into account whether the kitchen is equipped with only a single-bowl sink that might not be acceptable to many people unless a dishwasher were available.

The easiest places for an investor to overcommit are the range and the refrigerator. In a typical rehab apartment, a functioning range and refrigerator are all that is needed, unless they are eyesores. Then the investor should consider whether or not they would suffice if cleaned, given a new coat of enamel or paint, and polished up.

However, appliances may be money-wasters if they are inefficient, use more power than more modern appliances, and require frequent repair. Then consideration should be given to buying better, but not necessarily new, appliances. Be sure, in such an event, that the sources of energy that supply the apartment's old appliances can be expected to operate the new ones.

In regard to kitchen storage, adding cabinets can be one of the most expensive solutions to a problem situation. Look for a place where you can build a floor-to-ceiling pantry. All that is needed is a space that is as narrow as 3 feet wide, but that could be boxed in and fitted with ten or twelve shelves of varying heights to store different sizes of appliances and food items.

Cabinets can become very expensive, depending on the quality of the wood. However, they are important and cannot be overlooked in a kitchen that serves a large family. Consider though, that unpainted wood cabinets may be purchased for little cost at unpainted-furniture stores. They can be stained attractively and hung easily wherever needed.

Counters are another important element of the kitchen to be considered by the rehabber. The whole kitchen layout should be geared to providing the necessary surfaces near the sink and between the refrigerator and range, and 14 square feet of space is recommended for the average-sized kitchen. Preferably, at least 2½ to 3 feet of this counter should be set on each side of the sink. Above and below these surfaces should be sufficient storage areas to take care of the kitchen items used on a day-to-day basis.

Laminated plastic counter tops cost little and wear and clean well. They can add both to the cosmetics and the tenants' acceptance of the kitchen. They also represent an item that most rehabbers can do for themselves. Contact cement is the adhesive normally used for laminated plastic, and the big job of laying it down is to be sure it is cut to size. It is a hard material that needs a fine-toothed power saw or router for cutting if your hardware store cannot do it for you or you cannot buy the size needed, already cut.

Most kitchens that are as much as 10 years old are inadequately wired for the number of appliances that the typical tenant uses today. Therefore, it will be necessary to employ a licensed electrician to boost the capacity of the wiring system. Local building departments usually require that electric work be done by a licensed electrician and conform to the National Electrical Code. In some cases involving an increase in electric capacity, the replacement of an existing fuse box or circuit-breaker panel with one at a higher capacity and the addition of a special-purpose circuit for each piece of equipment may be necessary. Costs will vary, but boosting the service equipment capacity might run $300 to $400, and each special-purpose circuit might add as much as $40 to $50.

One of the failings that most disturbs a tenant is when the power goes down in the kitchen. Such a power drop can cause food in the refrigerator to spoil or interrupt the process of preparing food. Therefore, ask present tenants what power problems they have had. If they are recurrent, the cost of increasing electric capacity will usually have to be borne.

It is not a cost you want to bear if you do not have to because it does not add anything to the value of the building. It is expected that apartments will have adequate electric capacity. Unfortunately, in older buildings, kitchens frequently do not.

The items one finds in a luxury kitchen, such as a microwave oven, garbage disposal unit, frost-free refrigerator, exhaust fan, and cooking island, are not recommended for a rehabilitated unit. They may be expensive to operate, such as the frost-free refrigerator, or expensive to buy, such as the microwave oven. An exhaust fan should be provided and may be required by the building code if there is no window in the kitchen. It keeps odors from spreading through the building and cuts down on repainting because it reduces grease buildup on the wall.

In decorating the kitchen, opt for light but conservative colors in the wallpaper, floor-covering, counter-top, and appliance colors. Consider the lighting and how it could be improved at modest or no cost. Fluorescent lights are a good investment. Give this very important room an open, light feeling because it is a work place that can be drab and depressing to the family member who spends a lot of time there. Such drabness may cause tenant dissatisfaction that could be avoided.

If the kitchen is large enough, consider building a counter for having meals there. A market consisting mostly of singles or couples without children appreciates this touch enough to look for it and perhaps insist upon it in making a rental decision.

MODERNIZING THE BATH

The bathroom is the next important area after the kitchen for committing rehabilitation energy and resources. Look at your market again before you start. Assume that the market for the area consists of older (but not retired) couples or couples with children, who demand more than one bath. If there is only one bathroom, consider how you might either add a second or a half bath or at least compartmentalize the one bathroom so that a two-person household could use it more efficiently.

Adding a bathroom is an expensive proposition, even if you can find space adjoining the existing bath so the plumbing hookups are minimized. Only add baths if you plan to hold the property for at least 5 years or if the market for two-bath units in the area is so strong that you could charge significantly higher rents to help offset the expenditure. Resale of the property will gain back the cost of the improvement and more only if the rents can be set at a level high enough to improve the net income to a profitable degree.

Assume, for example, that the addition of a second or half bath gives the apartment additional appeal to couples who mainly populate the neighborhood. The addition of the second bath might cost $4000, but, if the rent of the apartment can be increased by 20 percent, for example from $200 to $240 a month, then the addition might be worthwhile. The reason is that the extra $40, amounting to $480 a year, capitalizes out to $4800 at ten times the annual net income with little increase in expenses beyond construction cost.

This illustrates an important point: many home improvements are said not to pay for themselves at resale. That is true in the case of a single-family home. But, for rental property, if the improvement adds enough to the apartment or house that higher rents can be charged, it often makes sense to do it. This is because the buyers of rental property purchase a building on the basis of its income, not on the same basis as the single-family unit that usually is purchased as a personal residence.

Thus, if the income is raised by $1, the next buyer might pay $6 to $10 for that $1 increase. Recall the basis on which you selected the building in which to invest. It was what return the building would provide after all expenses had been deducted from all income. That is the way you figure return on the property, and it is the way an investor who buys from you will figure it.

It is always, then, worthwhile to make an improvement that will boost rents to the level of other buildings in the area, so long as the improvement will bring in enough extra rent to justify the cost. The simple way to judge whether the improvement is worth doing is to multiply the amount of additional rent it will bring, minus the additional expense it will require to operate.

For a bathroom, the additional cost beyond construction would be the water, electricity, and maintenance required—probably about $5 more a month. If the rent increase amounts to $20 a month, the net income from the addition will be $15 a month, or $180 a year.

122 | REHABBING FOR PROFIT

Remember also that, on resale, you can deduct the cost of the bathroom from any profit made on the building. It represents a cost of upgrading the property that is deductible from income for tax purposes, as are most other expenses of operating investment real estate.

The decision as to whether the addition of a bath is feasible may be dictated more by the physical property than by the market. That is, there may be no way to put a bathroom in a logical place in a home. But, if there is one large bath, consideration can be given to dividing the shower and bathtub area from the toilet and washbowl (Figure 9–2).

A sliding door or a roll-back divider might be utilized to give one member of a family access to the area where one can apply makeup or shave, while allowing another person to bathe. Usually, such an arrangement is an improvement that would appeal to a couple that both work or a family with one child and only one available bath.

The investor wants to create an attractive bathroom that is also functional

**Figure 9–2 Two sinks expand the bathroom for a market that includes children.
(Poggenpohl.)**

without great expenditure. Sometimes, the big problem in the bath is an unsightly sink. Examine the sink to see why it is an eyesore. Maybe it only needs the replacement of outdated faucets, plus a thorough scrubbing to remove mineral deposits or other stains.

The sink might also be salvaged by building a cabinet around it or buying a cabinet into which it would fit. This would add desirable counter space, hide pipes, and provide storage beneath the sink.

A wooden frame around an old bathtub might also serve several positive purposes at little expense. When covered with laminated plastic or ceramic tile, the frame would provide a surface for bathing objects, help the decor, and save the $200-plus cost of a new tub.

Replacing faucets is an inexpensive improvement that can also help save water. By putting a flow adjuster between the shower head and arm, a flow of only 2 gallons a minute instead of the usual 5 gallons a minute can be achieved. That saves water and the cost of heating it and supplies all a tenant really needs.

An old-fashioned sink with separate handles for hot and cold water should be replaced with a single-handle faucet that adjusts for hot and cold water. There is definite market resistance to a sink that does not supply a faucet so that hot and cold water can be mixed to a desired temperature.

The bathtub that is showing wear and tear might also be rescued by installing a shower enclosure and extending the enclosure to the floor by building a wooden or laminated-plastic partition across the front of the tub. The enclosure should serve to keep moisture off the floor outside the tub where it does damage to the floor surface.

Ceramic tile is an asset to a bathroom unless it is full of cracks and leaks that are allowing moisture to damage the wall. Look closely at the caulk between the tiles and see if the old caulk might be scraped out and replaced. Even without exactly matching the color of the old tile, new tiles can be found that are close enough in color so they look acceptable as replacements.

A toilet that works poorly usually needs but the time and materials of a plumber. If the toilet is unsightly, thorough cleaning and the replacement of the seat may make it acceptable. When it is necessary to get a new toilet, ask the dealer about water usage and try to get the one that does the job adequately with the least supply of water. The older toilets use substantially more water than newer models, a consideration that will be a cost factor over a period of time.

The bathroom needs at least a duplex electric outlet to accommodate the hair dryers, electric razors, and other grooming devices that are commonly used today. Another outlet to power a heater might be necessary if the bathroom does not get enough direct heat in winter.

OTHER IMPROVEMENTS

After the kitchen and bathroom, the size of the rooms ranks high with prospective tenants. Guided by the market in the area, look at the rooms as if the walls between them did not exist. The bane of the investor in many old houses is the tiny room, so unpopular with many segments of the market.

Consider combining two of these small rooms, but only if the indicated market seems to be people who do not require the separation of rooms. For example, if the market consists mainly of couples without children, it might be much more appealing to this group to have one large bedroom with a sitting area than a separate but cramped bedroom and den. This arrangement might also be preferred by a market of retired or older couples without children, especially if extra storage could be provided as the rooms are combined.

Another solution might be to break out the center part of the wall between two rooms and replace it with a sliding door. This accomplishes the purpose of giving the tenant a bedroom connected with a sitting area at one end, so there is a feeling of spaciousness when the door is open and of privacy in each area when it is closed.

Rehabbers who go to the expense to change room sizes by combining—or in some cases separating—space usually do so with the advice of an architect or contractor to be sure they are not getting into something that would damage the structure of the building. But, it can be a worthwhile and not very expensive improvement if the market calls for it.

The combining of two small rooms will be more difficult, if not impossible, if the walls between them provide support to the house. These partitions are called "bearing walls" because they bear the weight of the roof or an upper floor. Nonbearing walls can be removed easily, but, to take out bearing walls, something such as a steel beam must be substituted to carry the load.

If combining rooms means putting in a beam, it probably is not worth the expense, which can be considerable. Ask a carpenter or contractor in the early stages if you plan to break into any wall and are not sure whether it is load-bearing.

Even in a nonbearing wall, electric wires, water pipes, and heating lines may be in the way. They have to be considered and avoided in breaking into the space. Some rehabbers handle the work of knocking down walls themselves, using a sledgehammer. It is not hard. Just wear a mask to keep the plaster dust out of your nose and mouth.

Knocking down a wall can be accomplished in a couple of hours if there are no pipes or wires in the way and you know where the studs are. By cutting into the wall with a jigsaw, you often can peer inside with a flashlight and locate the studs, pipes, and wires. Then, by sawing along the edges of the stud, the wall comes down without the necessity of using a sledgehammer.

If the partition does turn out to bear the weight of the roof, consider just adding a new entryway between two small rooms. Sometimes that will solve the problem of opening up an area of the house, especially if one of the rooms serves as the master bedroom and the other as a den or sitting room.

In looking at your floor plan, always consider how more storage space could be added, particularly if the market consists mainly of people past the age of thirty, whatever their circumstances. By that time, they have accumulated enough objects to want to store them somewhere—enough dishes, linens, clothes, books, papers, and mementos.

The addition of a closet need not be an expensive improvement. Look for space that the tenant probably would not use for furniture. Search the basement or attic for areas that could be turned into storage lockers or closets that would be assigned to each tenant.

The easiest addition to storage space consists of utilizing the existing space better. Some closets have poor shelf and clothes-hanging arrangements. Perhaps the simple process of adding shelves above or below those that exist or moving the clothes pole up so that a second pole could be added below would add substantially to the space.

Any unused space in the apartment might become a closet by imaginative carpentry or simply the addition of a sliding or bifold door and the construction of a few shelves.

In basement or attic, even areas that are likely to be subject to moisture or extreme heat can be converted to storage for some types of objects. Or a dehumidifier can be added to reduce moisture or a fan to reduce heat if storage is important enough to tenants and the apartments themselves do not provide any space to increase storage areas.

If the building has a garage or even a carport, do not overlook that possibility for storage. Shelves or cabinets usually can be built above the roof level of autos, and sometimes a whole wall of storage can be added along the rear of the garage. It may be necessary to insulate the garage to provide this kind of storage space, but the expense may be worth it if nowhere else is available to expand.

Again, the market for your rehabbed apartments is the key to whether the addition of storage space will pay off. Young couples with no children and both working probably can do with a minimum of storage space. Couples with children or older couples will seek a building that delivers on storage.

Next, the investor wants to look at the way the building is heated, with particular attention to whether separate furnaces with individual meters might be provided for each apartment. The cost of putting a forced-air gas furnace in an apartment might run as much as $5000 per unit if it also provides air-conditioning. But, that might be a better investment than running a big, powerful furnace for the whole building and charging tenants through the rents for heat. With separate meters, the tenant becomes responsible for these expenses.

There are good reasons to make this type of investment if you plan to hold the property for some years after rehabbing it. The cost of heating (and perhaps cooling) the building would be deducted from the expenses to operate the property, because that cost will be borne by the tenant. All the building owner must do is change the filters on each furnace regularly and have them inspected about twice a year.

Tenants in the apartment tend to use less fuel to heat or cool because they know they are paying for it. Thus, they shut down the equipment when it is not needed. With one central furnace, it is usually necessary to keep the equipment working 24 hours a day, which tends to wear it out.

Another advantage to separate heating and cooling units is that, if one breaks down, all tenants in the building are not inconvenienced. One furnace supplying heat to a whole building makes for unhappy tenants when it goes down.

The only places where the investor must supply heat, if there are individual units are the common areas. And, even hallways and stairways between apartments gain enough heat escaping from the individual units in the building to stay warm if good insulation is provided. While it may be desirable to add a small heater or fan in common areas, that expense usually is not necessary.

Making such a substantial investment as putting individual furnaces in apartments makes sense only in these circumstances:

- If the investor plans to hold the property for no less than 3 years. Though some rehab investors claim that they get their investment back in as few as 2 years owing to the relief from almost all heating and cooling expenses, 3 years is a more normal period. (On the positive side, remember that, as you reduce expenses, thus increasing net income, you add value at a rate of six to ten times the gain created by an improvement that achieves that result. Thus, a $20,000 expenditure on individual furnaces for four units that adds $5000 a year to net income through total fuel savings might be worth $30,000 to $50,000 to the next buyer of the property because he estimates the value at some multiple of the net income.)
- If the furnace is old and inefficient. Furnaces that burn oil instead of gas figure to increase most in operating cost. There may even be difficulty in obtaining the necessary supply of fuel. Therefore, the investor especially should consider going to individual fur-

naces in each apartment if oil is the source of fuel and the furnace is unlikely to last many additional years anyway.
- If the building has uneven heat that tends to build up in some areas and flow inadequately in others. Sometimes, it is just a matter of adjusting valves and dampers to correct this situation, but, in other cases, the problem is more complex and needs expensive ductwork to correct.
- If the building really needs air-conditioning because of the geographical area of the country or the way it is constructed or the demands of the market. Of these three reasons, the latter is the most important, though it usually reflects the first two reasons.

In some areas of the country, air-conditioning is expected, and a building without it is penalized in rents. Some buildings that are constructed like fortresses also retain heat like fortresses and cannot compete for tenants because of that fact.

However, when air-conditioning is considered, try first to determine if the individual units could not be cooled adequately by less-expensive room air conditioners. Many tenants in small apartments only ask for air-conditioning in one room—usually the bedroom. Giving them some escape from the heat without having to air-condition the whole apartment might be worth the expense of a reconditioned room unit or even a new one.

The company that supplies the energy you will use to heat and cool should be consulted as to what could be accomplished and at what price if any of the above conditions prevails. The company will send out a representative to make recommendations and offer a rough idea of the cost on the spot. Then, it is a matter of reckoning whether the return from the improvement would be offset by added rents and value.

The same advice applies for electric metering. It is highly desirable for each apartment to have its own electric meter and tenants to pay their own electric bills. Again, the investor is protected against increases and wasteful tenants by such a system. The electric power company in the area will advise about the cost of such a system.

In analyzing the merits of individual heating/cooling and electricity for each apartment, consider this probability: the rent level might have to be reduced somewhat so that tenants will be paying approximately what they would in a building that provided these necessities as part of the rent. Thus, if other comparable units in the area rent for $250 including heat and electricity and you would be asking tenants to pay $50 a month for the heating and electric expenses, then your own rents would have to be $200 a month.

But, to most tenants, that situation is more desirable. They would rather exercise their own control over these costs if they could pay substantially less in rent. Whether or not they do conserve energy, they believe they will. Therefore, the $200-a-month rent looks better than the $250-a-month rent. It probably will turn out to be a savings because a tenant who is paying all-inclusive rent tends to exercise little, if any, conservation. He figures, "Why not leave the lights on? The landlord is paying for the power."

So, it gives the investor a good competitive advantage to offer less rent, but to make the tenant pay the energy bills. Over the last few years, with energy costs soaring, such a system has made especially good sense. Landlords locked into 1- and 2-year leases with no escalation clauses for rising prices of fuel have seen their profits diminish enormously. Some even end up in the red until they can raise rents. Moreover, the size of the rent increases that were necessary to recoup from those losses caused strained relations with tenants that would not have occurred if the tenants had been responsible for their own energy bills.

The investor's primary objective in holding a building is to minimize the inflationary expenses and maintain the fixed costs. Thus, energy, maintenance, and labor costs are those that a property owner tries to transfer to the tenant, while accepting the costs that do not increase—mainly the mortgage payments.

In an inflationary economy, the original mortgage expenses will not go higher every month, but all the other costs of owning a building probably will. The investor wants to have the tenants pay for fuel and power, take care of their own maintenance if feasible, and even do some of the labor of keeping up the property.

In return, the investor asks for smaller rent increases than some other building owners in the area. This investor does not need the big rent hikes because the tenants are absorbing the costs that are rising—costs that force other landlords into the major jumps in rentals that lead to unhappy current and prospective tenants.

Whatever the source that supplies the heat or air-conditioning, keeping a building warm or cool depends almost as much on the way it is closed off from the outdoors as on the way the equipment works. Therefore, the matter of insulating the house becomes one of special concern to the investor who plans to hold a property for at least 3 years (Figure 9–3).

Insulation will not recover its value to the property owner until several years have passed, usually 6 to 10 years by government estimates. But, after 3 years, it will have produced some very visible energy savings that show up in the income statement for the property because it will have boosted net income by holding down expenses.

Remember that the buyer of a rental property looks at net income as the most important measurement of value. When a building is burning less energy, it makes a difference in net income compared with properties that are burning more. If energy consumption can be reduced 30 percent by insulation, it means

REHAB INVOLVING CONSTRUCTION | 129

Figure 9-3 Attic insulation reduces heating and cooling expenses and shows up to a good advantage on the balance sheet for a building.

that expense item diminishes the annual income by a significant amount. When the next buyer pays six, eight, or ten times net income for the property, that 30 percent saving is multiplied accordingly in the accepted value of the building.

But, insulating a building thoroughly is not recommended when an investor intends to hold the property for a short time or resell it immediately after rehab. No matter how conscious people are today of energy costs, the apartment renter rarely takes the matter of whether there is more or less insulation than another building into account. The typical renter will not pay much, if any, more for a building that is better insulated than another property that is comparable in all other ways.

Insulation is one of those hidden assets to which the market does not particularly respond. With some selling on the part of the investor or leasing agent, better insulation perhaps can bring a slightly higher rental, especially if the prospective tenant is older or retired. Then, the matter of a tight, draft-free building gains some importance. The tenant has had enough experience with buildings to know the difference in a well-insulated building and one that is not well-protected.

If insulation fits into your strategy, confine yourself to storm windows and doors in northern climates and insulating materials in the attic in all climates. These improvements are relatively inexpensive, durable, and practical.

Anything involving insulation in walls or "insulated siding," double-glazed or thermopane windows, or basement insulation probably will never be recovered from the savings it produces. These are long-term improvements made by homeowners who expect to live in the same location for many years. In fact, government agencies still cast sufficient doubt on the value of the materials that are used for wall fill that it would be a questionable investment at best to assume that current technology is equal to the job of reducing the heat loss through walls.

Plugging energy leaks is the cheapest and best investment. By applying caulking compounds to cracks and shutting off incoming air by weather-stripping, the investor goes a long way toward keeping undesirable heat or cold out of a building. About 40 percent of the energy waste in a typical building can be attributed to infiltration of air, almost all of it around windows that are not well-puttied and secure in their frames or doors that do not shut tightly (Figure 9–4).

Storm windows and doors achieve the same purpose of keeping outside air from the inside. Storm windows are more important because standard glass panes have poor thermal qualities. The extra glass protection of storm windows keeps cold from transmitting into the building interior through the glass while the frame of the storm window reduces infiltration. In warm seasons, storm windows may also help by reducing transmission of the sun's heat.

Less effective, but still worth the expenditure under most circumstances, are storm doors. A door does not transmit cold or heat as much as the glass

Figure 9–4 When a window is in such bad condition that it must be replaced, higher-quality thermal-glass windows may be a good investment. *(Andersen Corp.)*

surfaces of a window. It may be almost as effective to weather-strip a door well as to go to the expense of storm doors.

Buying storm windows and doors involves obtaining careful measurements of the space to be covered. The installation usually requires the services of a contractor recommended by the retailer offering the products. However, do-it-yourselfers who measure the openings carefully, and in accordance with what the manufacturer or hardware store suggests, may find the job within a layman's range of abilities.

Two more improvements that should be considered because they actually can, in some circumstances, add to income are the addition or expansion of a garage and the installation of a washer and dryer.

As always, the question of whether these amenities should be added depends on the market. Here are some reasons to consider adding a garage:

- If tenants are likely to be dependent on a car to reach a work destination owing to an absence of public transportation
- If shopping is too distant to be reached conveniently by any other means than an automobile
- If street parking in the neighborhood is difficult or dangerous
- If weather conditions are such that tenants need inside parking and will pay to get it rather than park on the street
- If the rents in similar buildings with garages are sufficiently high to indicate that net income would be substantially increased by the addition of a garage

In some areas of the country, a garage can bring in between $20 and $50 a month in additional income for each space. Either winter conditions are so bitter or on-street parking is so unavailable, that garage owners can rent their spaces, even if tenants do not take them.

After a garage is built, maintenance should be minimal. Therefore, almost all income earned by the addition of a garage applies to net income at the bottom line.

Expanding an existing garage might also be a desirable strategy. If two spaces are provided for a building with three tenants, who will more than likely have at least one auto each, the extra space might improve the rentability of the building at a better rate.

In some areas of the country, garage space is desirable but not so necessary that a tenant would pay much extra for it. In other areas, an indoor area for autos is almost essential. The investor must judge by the type of person likely to rent or purchase the rehabbed property just how necessary garage space is

132 | REHABBING FOR PROFIT

and whether the cost to provide it would be recovered in higher rents or resale value.

Few investors have the skills to build a garage, though it is a relatively easy construction job. Many contractors specialize in garages and advertise that specialty in the classified directory. One should take the same precautions in checking out a garage contractor with the lender, the Better Business Bureau, and local hardware stores or subcontractors as with other persons employed during the rehabilitation.

A comparison of price between garage contractors usually will not show much difference because the jobs are bid on about the same basis for similar buildings. (About $3500 is common for a one-car garage, with about $1500 more for each additional space.) The contractor usually has several plans to show a prospect and will obtain the necessary building permit. The investor should be careful to get zoning agency approval. The addition of a garage often requires a variance in the zoning for a property, though it usually is just a formality if the land area is large enough and proper setbacks and sideyards are indicated by the plan.

By the addition of a washer and dryer, the investor satisfies a definite need for tenants in many circumstances. For example, few young couples have purchased their own washers and dryers, so, if they are to be your primary market, the presence of such a facility can be important enough to pay extra rent for it. For any type of tenant who is unlikely to have a washer and dryer,

Figure 9–4 continued.

the investment probably pays off, especially if the nearest laundry is some distance away.

Coin-operated machines also can be installed under contract with a vendor. While the return to the property owner in these circumstances does not amount to much, the presence of the equipment on the property may be worth a few extra dollars in rents, and the return may pay for repairs and maintenance.

The investment in a washer and dryer that is not coin-operated will be worth extra rent, too, but these machines are notorious for breakdowns and service calls. With vendor-owned equipment, those service calls are at the vendor's expense, rather than the investor's.

Finishing an unfinished space, such as a basement or attic, can be justified as an investment only if it adds *necessary* living area or provides important new focus to a unit that has little or no character.

The cost also may be justified if the space can be finished with low labor costs and it is beyond reasonable doubt that the space will actually be used.

Finishing a space expensively when it will receive little use has been a common error of rehab investors. They think a beautiful basement will be so attractive to tenants that they will pay a considerable amount of rent above what similar apartments without that space could command. That does not often prove to be the case. There has been a consumer movement away from the use of a basement as a recreation area, especially if there are alternative rooms above-grade that serve that purpose.

National studies have indicated that homeowners who spend several thousand dollars to finish a basement or attic almost never recover the expenditure on resale. There are exceptions, and usually they occur when the units in a building do not include a den or family room.

Look at your market and potential costs very carefully before making this investment. Try to find other buildings similar to yours where the basement has been finished, and see how the last sale or rental compared to your purchase price or rent schedule.

Throughout this chapter, the emphasis has been upon choosing the type of rehab that makes sense from an economic standpoint. If no one will pay extra for an improvement or if the amount they will pay, compared to the cost, does not justify the expenditure, the improvement should not be made. (Exceptions are necessary improvements, such as work required to provide adequate wiring, heating, plumbing, and other services to tenants.)

Careful consideration of the probable market for a rehabbed property also must be given to each decision about an improvement. With the right improvements, done by competent labor at a fair price, the rehab investment should be ready to return a good profit to the investor.

How best to achieve that profit will be the subject of the final three chapters.

10 | RENTING FOR PROFIT

After the property is rehabilitated, profit is earned by doing one of two things: renting it for income or selling it to another investor.

Later chapters will discuss how to maximize the gain from selling the building or benefit through the conversion and sale of the individual apartments as condominium units. This chapter will be concerned with how to realize income and appreciation by holding the building as a rental property.

CHOOSING THE TENANTS

Critical to the possibility of obtaining the full investment potential of a rental building is the selection of tenants who will pay on time, maintain the property, and follow the rules set in the lease. Therefore, it is essential to screen prospective tenants carefully.

If the apartments already have tenants, get to know them as soon as you control the property—or even before, if possible. Ask them what is good and what is bad about the building. They will tell you a lot about the other tenants as they talk about the building.

Just by asking the question, "How are the other tenants in the building?" you are likely to get a line on which ones are not maintaining the property, which cause problems with noise, which are inconsiderate in their dealings with others in the building. All of these factors are important. It is the people who cause problems in a building that the investor wants to displace first in order to rehabilitate their units.

Take the complaints with a grain of salt, though. It may be the person doing the complaining who is the real problem, especially if the nature of his grievances sounds petty or vindictive. Weighing all the information gained from talking to the tenants can be useful, but one malcontent giving vent to his dislike of one or more of the other tenants should be taken for what it is worth—usually very little.

In talking to existing or new tenants, the investor who plans to live away from the premises should inquire as to whether the tenant would be interested in handling some of the on-property chores for a reduced rental. Perhaps a $25 to $50 reduction in the rent would relieve the investor of having to worry about yard maintenance, snow removal, common-area cleaning, leaf raking, and even rent collecting.

If the rehabilitation unit is a single-family home that the investor wants to rent, it becomes even more important to be selective about the renter. All the income from the property is coming from that tenant. Therefore, vacancy or collection problems can mean a 100 percent loss in income until the property is occupied again by someone more reliable.

Bringing desirable prospects into the building first requires a plan to reach them. Again, study the market for the area. What type of people seem to live there? What groups would be interested in the unit you have to rent?

Then, consider what these people read, where they shop, what services they use in the area. That is where you want to advertise your apartment.

Some grocery stores, drug stores, laundromats, and other merchants in the area provide free bulletin boards, on which apartments for rent often can be posted for little or no charge. The major employers in an area also provide such a service. Make neat cards, or have some printed, that offer your apartments for rent, and you will have a good chance of reaching the people who are most likely to come take a look.

Community newspapers often represent a better advertising buy than metropolitan newspapers. You can place a large ad there for less than a small ad in a larger newspaper. These newspapers also are distributed in the prime area where your best prospects live because most people tend to stay within a few miles of where they previously lived when they move.

Each community usually has a daily paper that is the real estate marketplace for most of the housing activity in the area. The paper is characterized by a large section of classified ads that people who are in the market turn to for a variety of choice.

Make sure your choice stands out among these many ads. Look at the other ads of a similar nature to yours, and select several that appeal to you. Then, try to write yours in a way that combines the best features of each. Classified advertising departments of newspapers will help write the copy, if you need assistance. But, just following the style of other appealing ads can be a good way to handle the matter.

Be sure the ads, whether classified or posted, carry this information: location, number of bedrooms and baths, conveniences, date of availability, rent, and daytime and after-work phone number of the person responsible for showing the building.

Selling starts with the telephone calls that will follow the appearance of an ad. A small sales pitch on the location; proximity to anything desirable; recent rehabilitation (including any new appliances); any concessions, such as the tenant's ability to paint or select carpet to his color choice; and other virtues of the property should be mentioned on the phone.

Ask the prospect some questions too:

"Do you work in the area?" (To learn where the prospect does work, if not in the area.)

"Is this size apartment right for your family?" (To find out how many people would be living in the apartment.)

"Are you living nearby?" (To get an indication as to whether the prospect lives in a lesser, equal, or better building.)

If the prospect shows an interest, ask further: "When can you come to see the apartment?"

That question is important because you will want to be sure an existing tenant is notified that the apartment will be shown. If there is no existing tenant, it still gives you a chance to be sure the apartment is ready to show.

Furthermore, sad to say, there is a security problem involved in showing a building to a stranger to whom you have only talked on the telephone. You may wish to have a friend present, especially if there are no tenants on the property and the area is still unsettled in character. If the caller sounded suspicious on the telephone by withholding or delaying answers to questions about employment or current address, be especially careful.

(In fact, it probably would pay in any case to call the employer or check the phone book to see if a person with that name indeed is employed or in residence where he or she indicated on the telephone.)

In showing the property, again emphasize its best features and the fresh, clean look of the unit. Point out how many people are moving into the area because of the great amount of upgrading going on there. Mention any conveniences, such as anything useful that is within walking distance. If the prospect has children, note the number of other children in the area, the proximity to schools or playgrounds, or anything else that might be attractive to them.

Most rental markets in areas where rehabilitation is occurring are strong enough that the investor should not have trouble filling the units. That is because the areas are well-located and the rents are below those of units of similar size in other well-located neighborhoods.

If you do have problems, however, there may be several reasons why. For one thing, your rents may be too high for an area where there may still be market resistance because renters have not recognized yet that a turnaround is occurring. It may be necessary to lower rents until the improvement in the area is detected by more prospective renters.

The problem may also demand more aggressive efforts to rent than you can make. Then, it is time to consult one or more brokers. Ask whether they have current rental prospects or good responses to their ads, and let them handle the leasing if their answers sound promising.

Sometimes, brokers can get action just by putting signs in their windows, listing available rental properties. They also advertise what they have available in the newspapers and show prospects more than one possibility at a time. If your unit is competitive in price and rehabbed appearance, it should stand such a comparison.

A broker will, of course, charge a fee for renting the apartment—a half month's rent or a minimum of $100 might be expected. So will apartment locator services that act as go-betweens for renters and apartment owners in many cities.

An investor definitely should try first to rent the building through his own devices. However, if nothing is happening, it may be necessary to seek professional help to get the apartment filled.

One final ally in filling the building, if they like living there, are the current tenants. By offering current tenants a half month's rent for a new tenant, you might save a lot of advertising costs and brokerage fees. The tenant is likely to recommend a friend who will check out as well as the tenant did.

In all cases, it pays to have applicants fill out a form, such as the standard credit reference form available from stationery stores or from your financial institution. Then, check the applicant out. Do not just size up the way the applicant dresses and acts and the stated income level and decide that this one looks okay and seems to be a nice person.

Management experts recommend calling the tenant's recent landlords, as listed on the application, but not the current landlord. The current one has a personal interest either in getting rid of a bad tenant or trying to keep a good one. The call might give the current landlord a chance to unload the tenant on you by a *good* recommendation or try to talk the tenant out of moving, while perhaps giving a *bad* recommendation.

Previous landlords have nothing to gain or lose and will answer questions such as:

- Did the tenant pay on time?
- Did the tenant leave the apartment in acceptable condition?
- Did the tenant cause problems with other residents of the building?
- Were there any special reasons why the tenant moved?

The employment record should be studied, too, for signs of stability. The personnel officer or some other officer of the current employer should be willing to verify that the employee works there and indicate the compensation paid.

Up to this point, the investor/manager has only invested a few minutes in making several phone calls to check out an applicant. As a final measure, though, if everything looks good up to that point, it might be well to run a credit check. The cost might be $50 to $100 for a local agency, but it will give you an idea how well the applicant maintains payments to local department stores, banks, and other creditors.

This step may not be necessary if previous landlords and employers have given favorable reports. But, if there is some doubt, a credit check is worthwhile to clear up doubts.

The accepted applicant should then be offered a lease. The format of the lease is so standard that virtually the same document is used for all rental property, and it is available from a stationery store or the office of the local real estate board.

But, how long a lease term to offer is debated vigorously by investors in rehabilitated properties. Here are the schools of thought:

- The longest that a lease should extend is 1 year because the investor must be able to raise rents within 12 months as expenses go up.
- A 2-year lease is ideal because it makes it unlikely that you will have to go to the expense of finding a new tenant after 1 year. (Some investors even opt for a 3-year lease, with an escalation of rent after the first or second year.)
- A short lease that continues month-to-month after the expiration period, unless the landlord or tenant gives 30 days notice, is favored by some investors because it enables them to evaluate a new tenant to decide whether that tenant is desirable for the building.

The circumstances of the building should determine which of these schools applies. If the net income is likely to fall because there is no way to pass heating, cooling, and electric costs through to tenants, then a shorter lease that can be rewritten at a higher rent in 6 months to 1 year is preferable.

On the other hand, if the tenants pay their own utility costs and property taxes are unlikely to be raised by a large amount, then a 2- or even 3-year lease might be favored.

It does cost a substantial amount to replace a tenant. There are cleanup and probably paint-up costs, advertising costs, personal time spent in finding tenants and arranging the move-in and move-out, and very possibly a loss of rent dollars if the new tenant cannot move until a month or more after the property becomes available.

Therefore, when the investor finds good tenants, he should do everything within reason to keep them. One way is to lock them into a lease.

However, an escalation clause should be added by at least the end of the second year and preferably at the end of the first. It might only be a small escalation, perhaps 5 percent if that is all you feel that the tenant will accept.

But, the whole object of holding a property is to increase the net income. Allowing a tenant to go for more than a year without a rent increase undermines that purpose, even if the tenant pays for most of the inflationary cost increases.

When a good tenant indicates an intention to move, find out why and try to accommodate him. If he wants to improve his interior space, offer to buy the paint and hardware. If he wants an air-conditioned apartment, offer to spend the necessary amount to install room air conditioners and/or fans that will cool the apartment in return for rent increases that will amortize the costs over a couple of years.

In short, keep in touch with the tenants that you want to keep in the building. Find out what will make them happy, and, if it is reasonable, try to work out a way to accomplish it.

MANAGING THE PROPERTY

One thing that makes tenants happy is a building that works. That means doing preventive and current maintenance. When there is evidence that something is going wrong, see what can be done about it, and send in a repair specialist, or do it yourself, if you know how.

That is good management practice anyway. If you catch a problem in time, it can usually be fixed with less expense than if you wait. A leaky faucet or running toilet, for example, adds to water bills and only gets worse. Before a roof becomes a big problem instead of a small problem, it is wise to repair it.

"Stay on top of your repairs and you will come out better," says Chicago rehab investor Don Norton. "Preventive maintenance saves a bundle of money. Skilled labor charges more if emergency repairs are necessary. Anything you can do to avoid an emergency is a savings."

Not letting the property deteriorate also impresses the tenants. They will keep their own premises up better if they know the building is being operated the way it should be, instead of being allowed to decline while the owner ignores the problems.

When an emergency breakdown does occur, the tenant should have a list of repair people that the investor has checked out as to competence and price. The repairs should be handled by having the tenant call the maintenance company. However, the bill then is sent to the owner, not the tenant.

This system gets the job done in a hurry during an emergency, but prevents the tenant from making a deal with somebody picked out of the classified phone book. Control is maintained over these expensive costs because the owner provides steady business to the maintenance company and represents a customer who can debate an inflated bill from a point of strength.

SPREAD SHEET FOR SEVERAL-UNIT APARTMENT BUILDING

Month	January	February	March	April	May	June
Finance Charges and Fees						
First mortgage						
Second mortgage						
Principal						
Interest						
Property tax						
Insurance						
Legal fees						
Accounting fees						
Management fees						
Repair Costs						
Carpentry						
Electric						
Plumbing						
Paint-decor						
Boiler						
Glass/windows						
Remodeling						
Other						
Monthly Expenses						
Electricity						
Water						

Heat/fuel
Exterminating
Garbage/refuse collection
Sewers
Miscellaneous
Auto
Appliances
Landscaping
Telephone
Advertising
Petty cash
Refund security deposit

Managers of small investment buildings recommend establishing a spread sheet of all the items of expense, with new figures added for each item every month. Any item that has grown significantly will show up at a glance. Thus, if water costs suddenly jump in a 1- or 2-month period, the investor learns that there may be a plumbing leak or a tenant who is wasting water.

When all the costs of owning a building are set out in this way and compared month to month, trends can be spotted that help determine the size of rent increases and indicate where adjustments or repairs must be made. The form also provides an ideal record for income-tax purposes at the end of the year.

Look at the form again, and see how any of the costs might be reduced. Remember that a dollar saved on expenses adds a full dollar to the profit on the building now and six to ten times its worth on resale.

The value of considering how to manage each of these items to best advantage is so great that the next few pages will be devoted to a detailed analysis of each item on the spread sheet, though some of these factors may have been touched upon in previous chapters.

The first and second mortgages are fixed costs that should not vary up or down. Separating principal and interest categories mainly benefits the investor by establishing a quick basis for figuring interest deductions for the year. But property tax, insurance, and legal, accounting, and management fees have some give in them.

Consider first the property tax. It should have been evaluated when you bought the building to be sure it was not out of line on the high side. If you discovered such an overassessment by checking the building against similar properties, it is time to appeal.

That process starts in the assessor's office with a check of your own property records and those of similar buildings in the area. Bring a list with you of comparable buildings in your area, and ask for your card and the others—a service that the assessor must provide.

See if your own property is described correctly as to number of units, size of building and lot, and other items. Your deed will have this information for the property you own, and what the assessor has recorded should conform. Also, check the mathematics to see that the valuation was correctly figured.

Now, compare your property to the others that you consider similar. An easy measurement is the assessed valuation of a building divided by its square footage. If that is off substantially, then there is good reason to study the matter further and find out why. Maybe the buildings really are not that similar. Maybe one is better located than the other. However, a big difference in square-foot costs should not occur for buildings that are really alike.

The assessor can change the assessment on the spot if an error has been discovered. Also, you can ask to have the valuation of your property justified to you, in light of any evidence you can show that your property has been overvalued. So, discuss the matter with a representative of the assessor's office first, if you think you have a case.

Beyond the assessor, you have recourse to an appeal to the assessment review board in that community. There, you will receive a fair hearing, and, more often than not, if your evidence is reasonably persuasive, a reduction in your assessment. About three-fourths of all appealed assessments are lowered, so it pays to give it a try if you have anything on which to make a case.

Insurance costs do not vary much from one reputable insurer to another, but a few dollars a month might be saved by buying from the company that offers the cheapest plan. Do not skimp on the essentials, especially liability insurance of at least $300,000. However, most basic fire and extended coverage policies cover everything that is necessary except liability.

If you buy insurance for 80 percent of the value of the building, the insurance company will actually pay 100 percent of the replacement cost of any accepted claim. Under the peculiar formula by which insurance companies work, 80 percent coverage means 100 percent coverage. Anything less subjects you to a percentage payout in event of a claim.

For example, if a building worth $100,000 is insured for $80,000 and a fire occurs that causes $10,000 damage, the company will pay off $10,000. But, if the building is insured for only $40,000, the insurer will pay half the claim, or $5000, because you do not have 80 percent coverage of the full value of the property, only half that much.

Therefore, the important thing to remember about insurance is the necessity to increase coverage as the value of the building goes up so that you always recover in full when a loss occurs. Your insurance agent should keep you advised as to additional coverage needed from year to year.

Liability insurance is especially important for owners of apartment buildings because claims are rather common that tenants have been injured through the negligence of the owner in not advising them of some unsafe condition. The minimum suggested is $300,000. The first $1 million payoff on a liability claim occurred in 1963, and the next 15 years produced fifty more. The extra coverage amounts to only a few dollars a year and could be well worth it.

Legal fees should be a minor cost to the investor who has chosen tenants carefully so that it is not necessary to serve eviction notices, institute action to obtain rent payments, and sue for damages to the apartment. After the initial legal work necessary to acquire the building, the rare use of an attorney should not be a major expense item.

Accounting fees, on the other hand, will be an annual cost that must be borne. Tax records must be developed, depreciation figured, and all legitimate deductions claimed. Only a competent accountant can provide these services.

But, for your money, you should also obtain good advice, not just a tax statement. Try to find an accountant who knows about income-producing real estate and can tell you how to take better advantage of the tax laws to increase your return. A knowledgeable accountant may advise you, for example, to replace a roof in one year instead of another because it offsets income better in that year or to make installment payments instead of paying cash for a landscaping job in order to take bigger interest deductions.

To save money with the accountant, keep good records. Give the accountant everything that will be needed to work from in readily accessible form, so it does not take hours of going through your papers to find what is wanted. Those hours will cost you money.

Management costs should be minimal unless you hire someone to operate your building. (This book strongly advises the investor to handle management personally, to the extent possible.) However, some management help may be needed, and it should be purchased carefully. First, try to rely on a tenant for management assistance. The price should be less, and the tenant is on the premises to watch for problems and respond to them.

A management company might also be employed, especially one that handles several buildings in the same area. It will bill your tenants, collect the rents, deal with necessary repairs, and even arrange for yard care and snow removal, if the owner desires. The price can be negotiated on the basis of what you want the company to do.

The third alternative is to have management handled for you by the manager of another, probably larger, nearby building. This person might consent, on a moonlighting basis, to provide assistance to your building for a monthly fee. This cost will probably be less than a management company would charge and perhaps even less than you might have to pay a tenant.

Consider all three possibilities if you cannot manage your own building because you are too far away or do not have the time. But, it can be the difference between a positive cash-flow situation and a net loss to have to go outside for management. Therefore, hold the management cost as near to zero as possible.

All repair costs are difficult to control because when something breaks down, it must be taken care of. However, the investor should know someone with each skill needed to maintain a building in good repair who will give good service at a fair price.

If possible, the investor should seek someone who is handy in more than one category listed under "Repair Costs" on the spread sheet. For example, many building engineers can take care of an emergency power failure or a plumbing or boiler problem without calling in expensive labor. Try to find such a person in a neighboring building who will agree to come to your building if an emergency occurs and make necessary repairs.

Not only will the cost be less, in most cases, but the service will be more prompt. Even putting such a person on a modest monthly retainer—perhaps $25 to $50 a month, depending on how frequently problems occur—may be cheaper than trying to get electricians or plumbers to the property in an emergency and then paying the rates they charge for such service.

In such an arrangement, the skilled engineers (or janitors) will also be able to do carpentry, install glass when a window is broken, and handle painting and remodeling. If they cannot do it, they will know someone who can.

So, first look for a handy person who lives near the property. Most of them are happy to supplement their income by handling the relatively simple (to them) repair costs for a building, on a moonlighting basis.

If that alternative is not open, then it is essential to search out service people who will be reliable about answering calls, who will do the work right, and who will not overcharge. The matter deserves some time and effort because repair costs in an older building can be a major expense.

Ask the tenants about repairs that previously were made in the building—who did them and whether the work was satisfactory. Ask managers of larger buildings in the area, because they make regular use of these people. If that draws a blank, look up in the classified directory the names of companies in each category that are located nearby. (Nearby plumbers are most likely to answer a call on an icy morning when a pipe has burst.)

Then, visit the companies. Tell them your purpose in wanting to become acquainted with them. Tell them what type of equipment you have, and ask if they have replacement parts for the components of that equipment that are most likely to break down.

Ask for references and check them. Call the Better Business Bureau or whatever its counterpart might be, and see what complaints have been lodged against the company.

Get a good list and provide it to each tenant. As previously noted, it is all right for the tenant to contact the repair company, so long as all bills go to the owner. Usually, it is more convenient for the tenant to make the call. However, be sure the tenants only deal directly with repair companies when there really *is* an emergency. Otherwise, the investor should handle the problem directly with the company and maintain control over time and cost personally.

Delaying repairs serves no good purpose and could result in additional damage and the need for more expensive repairs. When something breaks that you know will eventually need repair or replacement, get it done. The price is not going down, and it might cost more to wait.

Any repair work that the investor can do personally or with the aid of unpaid family or friends amounts to a saving, of course. Therefore, consideration should be given to reading the books that are available on simple plumbing and electric repairs, replacing broken windows, and other items that even the unhandy can follow instructions well enough to do. Remodeling, painting, decorating, and carpentry are other areas where the investor can save labor costs on repairs by doing the work personally.

Repair costs can be reduced by an investor who either does some or most of the work personally or employs someone who has the required skills, but not the overhead of the typical service company. However, it is a necessary cost of ownership that can never be avoided entirely.

Monthly expenses for electricity, water, heat, gas, and exterminating comprise the biggest expenses of ownership after the mortgage. They also represent the area that rises right along with inflation and may present higher and higher costs each year. The investor must exercise care that these costs do not exceed rents, so that the property becomes unfeasible as a rental building.

If you are lucky, most of these costs can be passed through to the renter by individual metering, especially heating costs. It has been previously recommended that the investor consider very carefully the cost of installing separately metered heating equipment for each apartment, instead of warming or cooling the building from a central system. If the costs are prohibitive, then the investor must take conservation seriously and try to hold these backbreaking costs to a minimum.

One way to conserve is to close all drafts that allow air into the building. Look around windows and doors especially closely, because that is where most of the cold air enters in winter and warm air in summer. A few dollars spent on weather-stripping can save more than its cost in one winter season, and it is an easy handyman's job.

Look at the entries to the building. Are tenants inclined to leave the doors open and let hot or cold air inside? Then, put a device on the door that will make it close automatically. They are available at hardware stores under various brand names.

Check out your lighting, especially the outdoor lights. Using fluorescent lights in a garage or outdoor fixtures can save money both on the tubes, which last many times longer than incandescent bulbs, and on power. Fluorescent tubes give five times more light, but burn less energy per watt, than incandescent bulbs.

Just reducing the length of time the outdoor and common entry lights are in use can also save money. Several timing devices are available to turn off lights at an appointed hour. It may be worth the price for one, especially if several lights are involved and the tenants are not inclined to turn them off when not needed.

The heating system often works inefficiently because it is not well-maintained or adjusted. One problem may be dirty or clogged filters that do not let the heat through, even when tenants turn the thermostat up. Filters should be checked or replaced on a monthly basis or at whatever frequency is recommended by the manufacturer.

Ask the utility company that supplies fuel for the boiler to suggest ways that the equipment might work better. The company will send someone for a free inspection if you indicate that you think you have a problem. Ask for proper settings and learn what adjustments need to be made during the year and how to get the most from the heating units in the building.

A boiler working at its best level of efficiency will save money. It costs so little to maintain it at that level that the investor should be certain that wasted fuel is not one of the unnecessary costs of ownership.

Combustion efficiency is what you are trying to achieve, and an annual inspection by a competent service company that measures this efficiency with special instruments can assure that you are getting the maximum output from the equipment.

Another area of efficiency to check is the setting of the hot-water heater. Anything above 120 degrees probably is too high, unless tenants start to complain. (That setting may not be high enough in some cases where pipe runs a long way before it reaches an apartment. But, it normally is good enough.)

Insulating hot-water pipes also will pay off in most cases by avoiding the cold pipes that cause the water to lose heat. The hot-water storage tank might also need insulation if cold air circulates around it.

Look at the common areas of the building—where you are responsible for heat, cooling, and light—and see if you can make some reduction in those costs. Maybe the hallway and stairway are too brightly lit or you are using lamps that are kept on all the time by tenants, instead of overhead lights that tenants would be inclined to turn off and on as needed by switches near the door and at the top of the stairs.

Perhaps heating or cooling the hallway and stairway really are not necessary for the comfort of tenants. Try it for a while and see what complaints arise. Often, the heat or cool air emanating from the apartments in a building prove to be adequate to take care of other indoor areas if the building is well-insulated.

Exterminating costs are difficult to reduce except by cutting the number of visits per year by the exterminating company or finding a company that does the job well for a better price. One of the most upsetting experiences for some tenants is to live in a building where there is poor insect control. Some buildings even get reputations as "roach havens." That is a reputation that no investor wants for his building. So maintain the exterminating service, but watch the costs, and check prices periodically with other companies in the field.

Garbage and refuse collection and sewer costs usually are levied by the local municipality, and there is little that can be done to effect material savings in this area.

Among miscellaneous costs of ownership, the owner can charge to the building the use of his auto for purpose of visiting the building to deal with problems there or show prospective tenants the property or for any other purpose that is relevant to the investment. The transportation expenses of trips to a financial institution, lawyer, accountant, or other person involved in the investment also can be charged as an expense to the building.

But, this item is shown on the spread sheet mostly to document the tax deduction. The way to reduce the use of the auto for this purpose, of course, is to handle more of the business involving the building by telephone.

Appliances may be necessary for snow removal, lawn work, hedge-trimming and other purposes. They can be depreciated annually over their expected lifetime, so that if an electric lawnmower can be expected to last for 8 years, one-eighth of its value may be claimed each year as a deductible expense.

Landscaping is a miscellaneous cost that can be substantial if the investor does not keep careful watch on it. Decide how to make your yard look as good or better than the competition, and quit there. Anything more will probably be expensive.

However, one way to get a better landscaped yard at little extra cost is to offer to buy the flower seeds for tenants who want to plant something that would add to the attractiveness of the exterior. That may be all the incentive a gardener, frustrated at living in an apartment building, will need to produce a beautiful addition to the grounds.

As previously recommended, try to find a tenant in the building who will maintain the yard, including shoveling snow, if necessary. That is the cheapest way to get the job done. The tenant is likely to feel a sense of responsibility to other tenants, as well as personally, to keep the yard clear and clean.

Failing that, look for other people in the neighborhood, or consider doing the work yourself. Many first-time investors find that the dollars they would expend to have someone else do yard work makes the difference between profit and loss in the early days of the investment.

Whatever the labor source, be sure the work is done. A building with unkempt grounds, burned-out grass, or weeds everywhere is not going to be attractive to present or future tenants.

Advertising costs should be mainly incurred in trying to find new tenants, and they can be minimized best by holding onto tenants or finding new ones at no cost. Both these points have been previously discussed in this chapter. Remember the free route of tenant referrals or apartment-for-rent posters in key locations should be tried before the apartment is advertised.

Especially advertising costs should be kept down in a good rental market. Using bulletin boards of local merchants and industry in the area to describe the apartment should be your first step when you know a unit will become vacant. The next step is to ask the departing tenant to recommend anyone who might be interested in the apartment. Also, ask other tenants in the building.

Then advertise. But, try the community newspaper first with a good-sized ad, as that will cost about the same as a smaller ad in the metropolitan press. Advertising costs should be a minor expense of ownership if the investor uses other means to obtain new tenants.

A fund must be maintained for security deposits that the lease requires to be repaid—less expenses for repairs to the apartment—at the end of the lease term. This fund should be in the form of a checking account or short-term notes that will pay interest.

It has become law in many states that the tenant must receive interest on security deposits. However, the law usually applies only to larger apartment buildings, not to buildings of one to six units. Therefore, use the tenants' money to make money wherever it is legal to do so.

To pay all of your expenses on time, with no interest charges, it is important to get tenants in the habit of paying the rent as soon as it is due. Experienced property managers recommend a system of supplying an envelope to each tenant 5 days before the rent is due, with the stamp and address of the party to be paid already provided.

That way, there is no excuse for the tenant not to write a check and put it in the mail by the first of the month, when the lease says the rent is due. If the tenant has not responded by the fifth of the month, another notice should be sent. A telephone follow-up may be necessary if there is still no check by the tenth of the month.

The investor's objective should be to have the tenants pay the costs of ownership. If the tenants are not sending the rent in on time, the investor may have to come up with personal funds to make payments to the electric company, the gas company, and other people who supply or service the building. That is not the way a smoothly managed investment property should work, so emphasize to tenants the importance of paying the rent promptly when it is due.

The purpose of all the cost-saving ideas put forth in this chapter is to accomplish one thing that is vital to the whole concept of a rehab investment: a better net income from the property. That net income is what supplies cash to the investor while the property is held and higher appreciation when it is sold. Put $1 more in that column, net income, and you may put ten times that amount into your pocket at resale.

11 | SELLING FOR PROFIT

ADVANTAGES OF HOLDING

Some rehab investors try to get their money back in a hurry by selling a property as soon as the rehabilitation work is completed. Unless financial circumstances dictate such a course, that strategy is not recommended.

The best way to realize the great investment advantages of real estate is to hold the property while inflation, demand for buildings, and improving conditions combine to create a much more substantial profit than can be realized by rapid turnover.

The tax laws also encourage holding the property. Many smaller income-producing buildings produce a negative cash flow, but the tax benefits give the investor some return by sheltering other income.

Holding the property in circumstances of negative cash flow might not seem to make sense when the investor could have the money in a risk-free savings account or government bond, earning a good rate of interest. But, when the added factor of property appreciation is taken into account, the investment becomes perhaps the best available to a small investor.

Appreciation does not occur overnight. Though rehabbing a building may persuade someone to buy it at a higher price than the investor paid, the work involved may not be worth the profit realized.

However, if the investor can improve the balance sheet so the all-important net income convinces another investor that the property is more valuable than the improvement created by the rehab job, the profit should be much greater.

Consider this example. A building is rehabbed at a cost of $12,000. The market now is willing to pay much more than the original $80,000 cost plus the $12,000 expended on the rehab effort. Assume that the market likes the property enough so that buyers are willing to go as high as $110,000 for the building, a neat $18,000 profit, minus closing costs and finance charges.

However, that profit requires the payment of taxes. Even at the favorable capital gains rate, a big chunk of the profit (25 percent or more) will go to the government.

On the other hand, holding a property sets up many possibilities beyond mere speculative rehab for immediate return. It could result in a deferral of taxes by exchange. Or, the investor might refinance the higher value to go into another investment. Or, the neighborhood might really boom as other investors complete rehab projects, and the value will escalate much beyond what the early rehab efforts accomplished.

Taking the above example, assume that rents are increased by 20 percent to a total of $1440 from a rent role at the time the building was purchased of $1200 a month. Expenses also go up, but, due to prudent management, the increase is only 10 percent, to $550 from $500. That means net income rises $190 a month, the amount that all income from the building exceeds all expenses (except mortgage payments, of course).

Assume again that buyers attracted to properties in that area are insisting upon a 10 percent return, and appraisers are using that amount to estimate market value on the previously discussed formula of net income divided by capitalization rate equals market value. That means annual net income in this example of $10,680 ($1440 income minus $550 expenses times 12 months) divided by 10 percent would mean a probable market value of about $107,000 ($106,800 rounded off).

But, let us assume further that after the initial increase in rents of 20 percent, the investor were able to add another 8 percent a year owing to the pattern of rentals asked and accepted in the area. Even if expenses went up the same 8 percent due to inflation, the investor would be gaining ground because 8 percent of the income is more than 8 percent of the expenses.

Thus, after 1 year, the 8 percent gain in rents would benefit the balance sheet in favor of net income by $854. That is derived by multiplying 8 percent by the $1440 gross income, then subtracting 8 percent of $550 a month in expenses, then multiplying by 12 months.

As the market now perceives the property after 1 year of ownership, if it still thinks a 10 percent return is appropriate for that neighborhood, the building has increased in value by $14,000 and now is worth about $121,000.

Consider this, however: As the market sees an excellent investment situation because the neighborhood is improving or the rental market is stronger, buyers might be willing to accept only a 9 percent return on investment property of this type. Look at what that does to the profit potential after 1 year in the circumstances described:

The property now is showing gross income of $1500 a month, or $18,660 a year. Expenses, also up 8 percent, now amount to $594 a month, or about $6128 a year, leaving $12,532 as net income. At a 10 percent capitalization rate, the property would be valued by the market at about $125,000. But, if investors will accept 9 percent, it would put a value of about $140,000 on the building.

That is why it is necessary in pricing the property to look beyond your own balance sheet to learn what is happening in the neighborhood. When the market begins to see good things happening in an area, there is a rush to buy there, and the rate of return that will attract investors diminishes. As investors become willing to accept a lower capitalization rate, property values rise.

It is important, then, to check recent sales to see what capitalization rate the purchaser was using. This can easily be done by dividing the net income by the price paid for the property. Your broker, who has probably handled some of these transactions, can show you several, so you will be able to keep in touch with how the market currently is judging properties like yours.

THE CASE FOR NOT SELLING

The above reasons argue that the best strategy is to hold for a few years. However, another point to consider is whether you want to sell the property at all.

Some rehabbers figure there is no way they will have a better long-term investment than the ownership of real estate. They improve a building and regard it as a life-time asset, gaining in value every year, providing income and tax shelter, and representing a lot of security for the retirement years.

They sometimes use an interesting device to hold the real estate even when they need the money available through appreciation in order to invest in other property. The method used here is refinancing, taking a new loan on the increased value of the property, while continuing to hold it as an investment.

Refinancing works best when there is very rapid appreciation in value, so that the investor can pull a substantial amount of money out of the property and use it for some good purpose elsewhere. It does not make much sense to take out a new mortgage if the interest rate will be significantly higher—more than two percentage points—or if the appreciation in property value has been less than 20 percent.

The reason is that the closing costs to arrange a new loan, the higher monthly payments, and the small amount of funds that can be gained from a property that has had a modest increase in value probably do not justify obtaining a new loan.

On the other hand, if the neighborhood has suddenly boomed, but the investor's property seems worth holding for still greater profit, then refinancing might be the right strategy. You get a new loan, which a lending institution will usually be happy to grant, and it covers 80 percent of the current value of the property, rather than 80 percent of the value when it was purchased.

Thus, if a building has appreciated from $80,000 to $120,000 and the investor has an 80 percent loan at the former figure—amounting to $64,000 plus some equity accumulation—the idea of obtaining a new loan that produces a $96,000 mortgage (80 percent of $120,000) may be appealing. As will be seen, it frees about $8000 to reinvest. But, it should only be appealing if the investor has somewhere to put the dollars gained in the deal.

The way such a transaction would work is that the investor would pay off the $64,000 mortgage; put down 20 percent of $120,000, or $24,000, to obtain the new one; and clear $8000, less closing costs and finance charges. These costs would probably be offset by accumulated equity from mortgage payments.

The important factor for the investor to determine before refinancing is whether the new investment contemplated for the use of the funds would return at least as much as the loss sustained by paying closing costs that might amount to several thousand dollars, plus possibly having to accept a higher interest rate. In most cases, refinancing is recommended only to pay off a second mortgage or consolidate several loans in a single mortgage.

CHOOSING THE TIME TO SELL

Investors who can choose the time to sell their property gain important advantages:

- They can study the market carefully over a period of time to see how strongly it appeals to renters and buyers. If renters of a higher caliber are coming into the area, willing to pay better rents for the location and improving facilities there, other investors will soon be there too, trying to buy buildings.
- They can constantly try to improve net income by raising rents and reducing or maintaining expenses. It is rare that a building for which income exceeds expenses by 50 percent cannot show some gain in net income each year, if the market will accept higher rents.
- They can look over the opportunities to exchange the property for something larger, so that they get into an investment with better return without paying any immediate taxes on the transaction.

The latter concept appeals to many rehab investors because it has enabled them to increase the value and return on their real estate without owing the government any taxes. These taxes are deferred until there is an actual sale, and, if the investor keeps exchanging property, or never sells, they do not have to be paid until some favorable arrangement can be made for transfer of the ownership through the investor's estate.

A good exchange market exists for real estate. People with bigger properties decide the time is right to look for something smaller that will not take the time or expense to maintain. Exchanging a twelve- for a four-unit building appeals to some people. Certainly, the owner of a smaller building should explore the opportunities to exchange for a larger one.

Deals between owners of large and small buildings also can be structured on an exchange basis by having a third party buy the smaller building after the exchange. The owners of larger buildings find it more difficult to market their properties because there are fewer people who can qualify to take on the large mortgages on these properties. Therefore, they exchange for a smaller building, then sell that building to the larger market available.

The investor with the small building gets tax deferral, uses equity accumulated in the appreciation of his building to swing a larger purchase, and perhaps assumes a favorable mortgage.

An easier exchange might be consummated with someone who owns a less-valuable building, perhaps one that has *not* been rehabbed in the same neighborhood. By offering your building and obtaining a cash settlement for the difference in value, you would have another property that could be rehabbed to realize the same return as the first one, and the cash difference would cover the cost of rehabbing the second property.

Exchanging real estate is a business in which some brokers specialize. They know all the tax angles and the names of some investors who like to trade and might be interested in your property. Ask around the brokerage and financial communities to see who especially understands the field of exchanging properties.

In the end, however, you probably will want to sell the property and take the ultimate gain from it. The timing should be planned so that you do not get out too soon or too late, which is easily said, but not so easily done.

The right time to sell real estate is when the opportunity for further gain seems to the investor to be less than the opportunity for reinvestment at a greater profit or when the risks in the market have increased more than the potential benefits of holding property.

These circumstances could occur if a neighborhood that has been in a strong upward cycle seems to have reached its peak, while a new area beckons with some interesting possibilities. It could also happen when the investor has drained every last ounce of fat from expenses, while resistance is developing to higher rents.

Good telltale signs are buildings that are offered for sale, but take months to find a buyer. Or increasing move-outs around the area, even though apartments still have few vacancies. The former indicates that the market may be asking a higher return in the area than recent capitalization rates indicated. The latter may mean that rents are getting so high that competitive neighborhoods are becoming more attractive than the area where the investor owns property.

In either case, neighborhood property values may be tapering off. Look at other neighborhoods, however, to be sure the trend is not larger than one neighborhood. It could be citywide or nationwide, due to economic conditions that cause investors to hold back on commitments and to seek less expensive accommodations (or to double up).

When you decide that the time is ripe to sell, consider first your own financial circumstances.

- Do you need all the money out of the deal now? If you can wait several years to get it all, you can use a device known as an installment sale that will significantly reduce the tax owed on the capital gain.
- Being able to wait also means you can take some or all of the action in financing the property, a great plus to the buyer. By holding the first mortgage or a second mortgage for part of the downpayment or perhaps even the first and second mortgages, you will establish a steady source of income without the burden of managing the property.
- If you do intend to make a clean sale, do you have another investment that is as good or better into which to channel the profits. (Maybe one rehab experience is enough for you, but real estate in general should be considered as a place to put the profits from a successful venture.) Selling just to meet current cash needs is not a good reason, if any other alternatives are available to deal with the cash-short situation.

The investor should look very carefully at the tax consequences of a sale and get the advice of an accountant as to how this liability might be minimized. The installment sale, for example, is a splendid device if mortgages can be avoided both by the buyer and seller—a rare circumstance.

The way it works is that the buyer gives the seller up to 30 percent of the agreed-upon price in the first year and specified amounts each year thereafter, while paying interest on the outstanding balance. Thus, the seller does not have to declare more than 30 percent of his profit in any given year, the buyer usually gets a lower interest rate than a bank would provide, and the deal can favorably affect the tax payments of both parties.

SELLING FOR PROFIT

The problem is that the seller must find some way to pay off the existing mortgage while only receiving 30 percent of the value of the property in any one year. From the buyer's standpoint, larger annual obligations must be met than from a conventional mortgage because the seller usually wants full payment within a few years.

Agreeing to hold a mortgage on the property often will help the seller get top dollar and bring in a steady income that is virtually risk-free. The investor's own previous real estate investment is the collateral. An offer of financing assistance, especially to reduce the buyer's downpayment requirements, opens up the market to many more potential buyers.

The danger is that the buyer in this situation might be irresponsible and allow the property to run down again. Make your own evaluation of the buyer, including a check of references. You are protected to some extent if you are offering a second mortgage on top of a first mortgage provided by a bank in that the bank also has checked the borrower out thoroughly before making the primary loan.

One vital fact that you need to know before you can make good decisions about how to handle the tax problem of a sale is just how much profit you have in the property.

First, make a simple subtraction of the amount you paid for the property from the amount you expect to receive on resale. Then, subtract from that number all documented expenses you absorbed in rehabilitating the property, but not in maintaining it. Any labor costs, paint and other materials, trees and shrubs, insulation, rewiring, plumbing, etc., that has not been claimed as maintenance on the tax form prepared for the Internal Revenue Service each year will qualify.

For example, if the property cost $80,000 and you spent $10,000 improving it, then sold it for $110,000, your tax liability would be $20,000. The rehab costs must be documented, however, with supporting evidence, such as receipts, invoices, and so forth.

Knowing your profit may help you make the right choice between holding and selling. The investor should realize that a sale costs money and will reduce the profit, especially if a real estate agent is employed to market the property. The agent's commission comes from the seller, not the buyer. So does a good portion of the closing costs, which could amount to hundreds, maybe even thousands, of dollars.

The brokerage fees, at least, can be avoided if the investor can sell the building without the aid of an agent. That means a savings of 6 to 7 percent on the sale. In the example of a $110,000 building, the cost to use a real estate agent would be $6600 to $7700, a stiff price to deliver to a broker after an investor has put in so much hard work to make a profit on an investment.

In some areas where properties are turning over well, there is no reason to use a real estate broker. Advertising the property is not so difficult, though it is not the same as advertising a house for sale. People who buy income-producing property want to know how many times net or gross income the buyer is asking, how much vacancy there is, and what level of rents the tenants are being charged.

Look at ads for other income property for sale, and try to emulate the best of these—the ones that would interest you in seeing the property advertised.

Again, put posters or smaller notices on local bulletin boards that are provided by merchants and industries in the area. Ask your own tenants if they would be interested in purchasing the property. Use display-size ads in community papers, as well as classified ads in metropolitan daily newspapers.

Prepare good materials to show investors who indicate an interest. The best document to offer them is your most recent tax return on the property if you want to be entirely honest about it. Most property owners do not want to go that far because they think they can get more by indicating income and expense ranges and showing as little documentation as possible. But, some kind of balance sheet must be prepared, and it would be more persuasive if the seller were willing to show by receipts that the information was not fabricated.

You can negotiate best with a knowledgeable investor when you can provide evidence of market sales in the area that indicate that your property is fairly priced. The prospective buyer probably already knows about those sales and will take them into account in an offer. But, it does no harm to present this evidence to show that you know what your property is worth and cannot be talked into an unrealistic price.

With no broker involved, the investor should have assistance from an attorney, both to assist in the preparation of the contract and to negotiate with the prospective buyer. The attorney should inform the prospect of any concessions that the seller has decided to make, such as taking back a second mortgage or reducing the price by a given amount.

Face-to-face negotiation is difficult for both buyer and seller. The buyer must knock down the property as not worth what is being asked, and the seller must defend it without getting offended over the negative points being made.

The broker handles all this; it is part of the fee. There is the added value that the broker wants both parties to compromise until they reach a point of agreement, so the commission will be paid. Therefore, the broker may come up with some ingenious ways to get around impasses.

Using a real estate agent also has the advantage that the broker usually knows investors who might be interested in a new property on the market. Remember how you used one or more brokers in buying? When new properties came along, they called and encouraged you to look the buildings over.

The same benefit accrues to the investor who puts his property in a good broker's hands (by now, you should know who the "good" ones are).

The matter of using a broker or trying to sell a building yourself really depends on your time and availability to concentrate on selling the property, whether the market is active or sluggish, and whether the advantages of having a broker outweigh the 6 to 7 percent cost.

Real estate rarely is offered at the price that the owner expects eventually to get. Therefore, you must start at about 10 percent above what you will accept and negotiate to get something near that figure, hopefully above it. An investor who has followed the advice in this book will know what the property is worth at all times through a periodic check on market sales, an analysis of how much return prudent investors expect in the area, and the ever-handy net income figure.

Thus, pricing the property should not be difficult. It would be well, though, if the investor were under no compulsion to sell if an acceptable offer were not made. Pulling the property off the market for a while to await better conditions might be necessary if the buyers of investment real estate still do not recognize the true worth of property like yours—as is often the case when a neighborhood is still stabilizing, but is not yet there.

Many other points about the steps involved in a sale of property and the procedure for concluding the transaction safely and fairly are covered in Chapter 2, "Choosing the Property," though they are described from the buyer's rather than the seller's standpoint. Review that chapter when it comes time to sell to recall how you proceeded to contract as a buyer because most of the points covered apply as well to a seller as to a buyer.

With the help of a good attorney, plus some advice from an accountant as to the possibilities of tax savings on a sale, you should realize a worthwhile profit from a rehab investment. Remember that it is a leveraged profit because most of the gain will be paid to the investor though most of the money was put up by a financial institution, the seller, or some other third party.

All that third party realizes out of the deal is interest payments for the use of the money. In a successful project, the investor realizes much more: tax shelter, appreciation, perhaps cash return, and personal satisfaction from having taken a declining asset and turned it into a profitable one.

12 CONVERTING TO CONDOMINIUM OWNERSHIP

Anytime an investor can rehabilitate a building and then sell off the individual units to condominium buyers, the prospect should be thoroughly explored.

In most cases, the combined sales of the individual units will amount to significantly more than the sale of the building as a whole. The parts of a whole are not supposed to equal more than the whole, but be assured that many investors have found that by offering the units individually, their profit has been greatly enhanced.

Condominium conversion has become an established way of profiting from a rental building in some major cities, even for buildings with as few as three units. Concerned by their inability to stay ahead of inflation by raising rents, apartment building owners have considered conversion as the best way to sell out and reinvest. Their net income, capitalized, would not result in nearly so high a sale price as the division of the building into its individual units and then their sale to condominium buyers.

Several important conditions should be present for a building to be convertible. First, the units after the rehabilitation should be more attractive than average apartments in the area. Generally, they should be a bit larger; have more amenities, such as dishwashers and air-conditioning; and have some special features—handsome woodwork, fireplaces, high ceilings, or up-to-date baths or kitchens. Then, they should be well-located, preferably in a superior location to competitive rental buildings. Finally, they should appeal to tenants who already live in the building so that one or more of the sales can be made to that market.

The ideal small convertible building is one in which the tenants have resided for several years and appear comfortable. If it can be pointed out to these tenants that they could buy their unit at a price that, with the tax advantages, would amount to less than their rent, it should be easy to arouse interest.

The fact is that small condo buildings, where the owners can maintain close control over common expenses, usually will cost about the same or less in monthly mortgage payments and maintenance charges than rents in a comparable apartment building. When the condo owner takes into account deductions for interest and real estate taxes, it usually would pay to own rather than rent the same unit.

Objective studies also have shown that condominium units increase in value at a comparable rate to single-family housing in many areas. Thus, the buyer of a condo unit makes a long-term, as well as a short-term, investment, and few have failed to realize an appreciated value if they held the unit for a few years.

BASES FOR CONVERSION

Here are reasons to consider conversion:

- If other condominium conversions have occurred in the area. Even if the other buildings are much larger, they set a precedent for the area, so that people will think of it for potential ownership as well as rental. Many people who like the idea of condominium ownership do not want to live in a large building where they lose all influence over the decisions made jointly by owners about maintaining their buildings. They look favorably, however, on smaller buildings where they share the control with only a few other owners.
- If other new condominium buildings are available or under construction in the area. In almost every case, the price for a converted unit is well below the price for a new unit of comparable size and amenities because the older building was constructed at a substantially lower cost. Converters often can charge 20 to 30 percent less for the same amount of space and equal amenities than the developer of a new building and still make a good profit. Also, the existence of a new condo building in the area tends to substantiate that a condo market exists there. At least, it confirms that a developer and his financial institution think so.
- If the area includes primarily individually owned single-family homes. Where ownership has been established and homes are being well-maintained, it makes sense to continue the ownership trend by converting apartment buildings.
- If tenants in the building like where they are renting well enough to want to own the apartment. The best way to find out is to ask. In some cases, the idea will already have occurred to the tenant or be a welcome suggestion.
- If the purchase rather than rental of a unit make economic sense

for the market in that area, that is, if it can be shown that the buyer of a condominium unit will pay less each month if the unit is bought rather than rented, the case for the economics of buying should be persuasive. But, the investor should also be careful that the market for the area really would be interested in owning. Young marrieds with children probably would not buy unless schools and playgrounds are nearby. Elderly people would not likely be buyers, either. But, singles need the tax advantages. So do young marrieds with both members of the couple working and no children.

- If the sale of individual units rather than the whole building makes economic sense to the rehab investor.

The latter point needs elaboration because many investors give no thought to the possibility that their building is worth more if its individual parts are sold separately than if the whole property is sold as one piece. Consider this example supplied by an investor in Chicago:

A building was purchased for $95,000, and another $25,000 was put into its rehabilitation. After the rehab work was completed, the building was at least the equal of the best in the neighborhood, perhaps a bit better. The building was a good one to begin with. It had just been allowed to run down. So the $25,000 brought it back to first-class condition, especially the kitchens and baths, and each of the four units was cosmetically appealing. Further, the building was operated well, as the tenants who moved into it found to their delight.

After about 2 years of full tenancy, with easy rent-up for any apartment that became available, the owner decided to see what the property would bring on the open market. It was listed at $168,000, based on the market's willingness in that area to pay ten times the net income of $3750 per apartment, or $15,000, a year, plus $18,000 for negotiating room.

The investor got enough nibbles to know the property could have sold at somewhere between $155,000 and $160,000. But, the number of conversions of larger buildings that had been rehabbed in the area and the prices they were getting for the same sized apartments convinced the investor that these units might sell off at about what the bigger converters were getting, especially if a little less were asked.

So, the investor verified the price of $50,000 for a comparable unit, reduced it to $47,500 for this building, and went to the tenants to see if any would be interested in owning the apartments with which they had shown so much satisfaction. If all four units could be sold at that price, the investor would make $190,000 instead of the $155,000 to $160,000 the rental building would bring.

As it happened, three of the four tenants were interested in buying, and one even wanted to buy the extra unit and maintain it as a rental investment. (The owner had thought of that idea too and planned to buy one of the units personally if the tenants had not responded so well.)

This case was unusual in that the investor never had to go into the market to find buyers, but was prepared, if necessary, to suggest to prospects that they look at the units and at the others that were available in the neighborhood. The investor knew that they would find that the competitive units were not as attractively rehabilitated as this property, and that the price asked for these units would be less than the price asked for units in other buildings in the area.

That is the key point to be aware of in a conversion: the market dictates the price of each unit, rather than the balance sheet, which remains the crucial factor in what is paid for a rental building. Almost invariably, the market price for an individual condominium unit will be higher than what that unit contributes in capitalized net income.

Thus, time after time, people who have owned appropriate rehabilitated buildings have done themselves and their buyers a favor by converting to condominiums.

WHEN CONVERSION WILL NOT WORK

It is an exceptional investment strategy, but only if the circumstances are right so that it can be done.

It cannot be done in some cases—or at least not without great difficulty. Here are the conditions under which it may not be possible:

- If the market is not familiar with the condominium concept in that area. When the only market is for rental apartments, it is usually fruitless to try to educate people to buy. Some areas will forever serve a renter's rather than an owner's market, and, if that seems to be the case in your area, it is difficult to fight it.
- If the building does not lend itself to ownership. Some buildings just were not meant to be converted. Their rooms are too small, the walls are too thin, the layout is wrong. People who would accept the idea of a short-term rental there would not think of buying their unit.
- If the economics do not work out for the converter. In the last case, selling all the units in the building might take so much time and expense that the investor would be better off to sell the building as a rental property or continue to hold it until condominium shoppers became more attracted to the area.

The economics of conversion depend on what can be obtained for each unit as determined by the market for similar condominium properties and how long it would take to find these buyers. If other buildings that convert in that neighborhood or a similar neighborhood take 6 months to 1 year to find buyers, the turmoil and financial drain might not be worth the price.

Your tenants, knowing your plans because they have been offered the units first, will move out as soon as possible and leave vacant units. The length of their leases might also prove a problem. You might be able to sell, but unable to let the buyers occupy the property.

Further, the attitude of lending institutions toward financing condominium units in the area might be negative. Lenders might take the attitude that the venture is unsound for one reason or another, usually because they think the neighborhood is not ready for small condominium conversions. Therefore, it is necessary to talk to lenders about what you plan and see if they would be willing to finance units there.

One more factor that should be considered is statutes or ordinances that might restrict conversion or make legal compliance with a government agency's "full disclosure" rules prohibitively expensive.

Typically, a community that is trying to restrict condominium conversion will require that a certain percentage of the existing tenants agree to buy their units before a conversion will be acceptable. The number is 35 percent in New York and 51 percent in Maryland (as of 1979), for example.

A few states and cities have simply slapped a moratorium on any condominium conversion. However, most of these cities have limited the ban to buildings of twelve units or more.

In the interest of full disclosure, some states and cities require that the converter supply a full engineering report on the physical state of the building.

A lengthy legal declaration establishing a condominium form of ownership must be prepared for each buyer or prospective buyer in virtually every jurisdiction. Most condominium ordinances also require that the converter supply a master deed, individual-unit deeds, and the bylaws of the owners' association. Though these are comprehensive documents, most are formularized, so that real estate attorneys will supply them at a reasonable price.

CONCERNS OF THE CONDO BUYER

If the investor decides to go the route of conversion, there will be certain fears among prospective buyers of individual units that are not common to the more sophisticated buyer of an entire apartment building and must be faced.

The principal concern is that the expenses of operating the building will soon require the buyer of the condominium to come up with a much greater outlay for what is termed the "monthly assessment" or the "common interest charges." These are costs that condo owners pay each month to maintain the building outside the owners' separate units—to keep up the grounds, light and heat or cool common areas, maintain the garage, provide insurance for the building, and build up a fund for replacement of various components and systems as needed.

The assessment worries people because there are many instances where it has increased greatly after the building was purchased, compared to the budget the seller showed for these costs.

The way to relieve the minds of tenants in this case is to show them your expense statement, either the one you prepared in buying the building or one that represents actual costs over a recent period of ownership—perhaps the last 2 years.

They should be able to tell from this information how rapidly expenses are increasing and what they would likely have to put forth in added assessment costs in the future. Remind them that if the building were not converted, the rents they would pay next year for units of that type would reflect the higher costs. In other words, most of the assessment costs now are hidden in the rent, and, as expenses rise in an apartment building, the landlord simply increases the rent to cover them.

A second concern of the buyer of a condominium is the financing. This especially is true of tenants already in a building who would like to buy, but cannot come up with the downpayment. This is the lot of many people who rent. They would buy if they had enough money to put 20 percent down.

Here the investor can offer to help, if so inclined. If you have a buyer who could qualify with a lending institution on the basis of salary, but who cannot raise the downpayment, it would be wise to agree to hold a second mortgage.

Be sure the buyer has at least some money in the property, but to offer a good prospect some help with financing should definitely be considered. For one thing, as had been noted, the sale of the units as condos brings in more money than would have been realized from the sale of the whole building. Therefore, the investor has extra money to play around with, and few investments combine the safety of such good collateral with the high interest rates of a second mortgage.

PRICING AND SELLING THE UNITS

In selling the units, you have the same two considerations as you would have in marketing the whole building—how to price the property and whether to sell it yourself or use a broker.

Some converters use a formula of 125 to 150 times current monthly rent. Thus, a unit selling for $300 a month would be priced at $37,500 to $45,000. But, it is necessary to check the market. That is a rather wide range, and whether to establish a price at the high or low end depends on the price other condo sellers are getting for similar units.

So, make honest comparisons with condominium units offered for sale that are as comparable as possible in location, size, amenities, and other factors. Then, put in an expense factor for time to rent; possible loss due to vacancy; advertising, legal, and sales costs; and other expenses; and see whether the whole concept makes sense.

Trying to sell the units yourself depends on how many of your tenants will buy and how strong the market for condominium units has been in the area. If half or more of the units are going to be purchased by tenants, you have some reason to believe you can sell the rest rather quickly. But, the advice and continuous effort of a broker might be worth the sales commission, even in the circumstances of having some sure sales, because an experienced condo sales agent can help with all the rather unique circumstances of the closing.

The likelihood or certainty of at least one current tenant buying should be considered highly important to the investor's decision to convert. It gives the assurance that the building has a market, and that a friendly source in the building will help make the condominium work.

It also is beneficial if the investor occupies a unit on the premises of the building. Some unit in the building must be shown to prospective buyers, and the building owner's unit is best for that purpose. If the owner intends to buy one of the units personally, so much the better. That is one less to sell, and it encourages prospects to know that the building owner likes the investment quality of the individual units enough to purchase one.

The conversion of a rental building to condominium is an everyday occurrence in many cities. It is something to be considered and analyzed in terms of the market as a highly profitable alternative to selling the whole building to another person, who might be planning to convert and take the profit that you should realize.

Get sound advice, however, because the processes of conversion are not nearly so uncomplicated as those of buying and selling a whole building or a single-family home.

GLOSSARY

Accelerated depreciation An accounting procedure that takes advantage of an allowable speedup of depreciation in the early years of an investment.

Agent, real estate A person who is licensed to sell real estate.

Agreement of sale A document containing provisions agreed to by a buyer and seller of real estate, stating essential terms and conditions.

Amenity An attractive feature of real estate that adds to the satisfaction of ownership.

Amortize To pay back a financial obligation by making regular (usually monthly) installment payments.

Appraisal A written estimate of the value of an identified property.

Appreciation The increase in value of real estate.

Assessed value The value of real estate as estimated by an appraiser for a taxing authority.

Assessment The charge made against an individual real estate parcel by a taxing authority. Usually some multiple of the assessed value. In a condominium, the monthly fee paid by owners toward the maintenance of common areas of the building and other expenses.

Assumption or assumed mortgage An agreement to take responsibility for an existing mortgage and pay it off on terms agreed to between another party and a lender.

Balance sheet A statement of the income and expenses of a property.

Balloon or balloon payment The final installment payment of a note, which usually is in a substantially greater amount than any preceding installment.

Building code Local regulations that regulate the construction quality and materials used in new construction or rehabilitation.

Capital gain The difference between the original cost of the property, with adjustments made in that cost for allowable improvements and expenses, and the net resale price.

Capital improvement A major improvement or change in real estate that adds to the life of the property or makes it more valuable.

169

Capitalize To compute the present value of real estate based on a multiple of income that would prove attractive to an investor in that type property.

Capitalization rate The specific multiple of income that the real estate market would expect as a return on an investment, based on other investment alternatives and a perception of the risk involved in the property.

Cash flow The amount of income remaining after all expenses, including mortgage payments.

Closing costs The various expenses of completing a real estate transaction, including the cost of a title search, attorney's fees, mortgage fees, and prepaid items such as taxes and insurance.

Collateral Property or assets offered as security for a loan.

Commission, real estate The fee paid to a real estate agent for services provided in the sale of real estate, usually 6 to 7 percent of the sale price of the property.

Comparable sales A measure used by appraisers and investors to compare properties of similar characteristics in order to estimate the value of real estate that is for sale by comparison with real estate that has recently sold.

Conditional contract An agreement to sell real estate subject to either buyer or seller fulfilling certain conditions that are stated in the contract.

Condominium A form of ownership in which individuals own specifically defined units of space in a multiunit building and share ownership of common areas outside that space. The term is used colloquially to mean the unit of space itself.

Constant The regular monthly or annual payment due on a mortgage over the life of the loan.

Construction loan A short-term loan to cover rehabilitation costs until a long-term mortgage can be arranged for the improved property. Disbursements are made as agreed by borrower and lender.

Contractor A person or company that agrees to provide services to rehabilitate or improve property for an established compensation.

Contract sale An agreement to sell property wherein the seller retains title to the real estate until all contract terms have been met.

Conversion The legal change in the ownership of real estate to a condominium form, usually from rental.

Cost approach A method of appraising property by estimating the actual cost to replace existing structures, minus depreciation, and plus the market value of the land.

Deed A legal document that conveys ownership of real estate.

Debt service Collection of interest on a mortgage loan, plus a portion of the principal owed.

Deferred maintenance Requirements for maintaining property that have been put off rather than fulfilled.

Deferred tax A tax liability that is not immediately due because government regulations permit payment at a later date.

Depreciation Real or tax-related deterioration. Tax-related depreciation does not

GLOSSARY | 171

reflect actual physical deterioration, but rather that allowance permitted by the government for assumed deterioration over the life of a building.

Easement A right granted by a property owner for the limited access to or use of property by another party.

Economic life The period of time in which a building will bring a return to its owner.

Economic rent An expected rent on a property that provides an economic return to its owner.

Effective age The age of the building in terms of its condition and likely remaining life, as opposed to its physical age.

Equity The value of a property less any debt.

Escrow A deposit of funds with a third or neutral party, pending the fulfillment of certain agreed-upon conditions. Upon fulfillment of those conditions, escrow funds are dispersed by the neutral party.

Exclusive listing An agreement with one brokerage firm or agent, giving exclusive right to sell a property for a specified period of time.

First mortgage The primary loan on a property, taking precedence over all others.

Foreclosure The legal process to take possession of real estate because of failure to comply with a contract or lease.

General contractor The person or company that agrees by contract to assume primary responsibility for construction work, with authority to employ subcontractors as needed for various aspects of the job.

Gross income The amount of money that would be realized if a rental property were fully occupied at economic rents, plus any additional income from the property.

Homeowners policy A package insurance policy available to property owners covering the dwelling and its contents for damage from fire or wind, as well as for theft and personal-injury liability.

Income and expense statement A schedule of all income and costs related to the operation of a property. Used by investors in buy-and-sell decisions.

Income approach An estimate of value based on the capitalizing of net income by a rate considered appropriate by the market for that type property.

Income-producing property A building that is rented to provide income for its owner.

Installment sale A sale designed to reduce the amount of capital gain in any one year by paying for property on a basis of no more than 30 percent in any year.

Interim financing A short-term loan to cover an investor's needs until a permanent loan can be arranged.

Interest rate A sum charged for the use of money.

Junior financing or mortgage A loan that is inferior to the first mortgage or to another mortgage that takes precedence.

Lease A contract under which one party allows another the use of property in return for the payment of rent and conformity with other specified conditions.

Lessee A tenant, or one who has the right to occupy property under terms of a lease.

Lessor A landlord, or one who grants the right to the use of property under terms of a lease.

Leverage The use of borrowed money to enhance an investor's return on equity. A loan in which the investor has no money invested is 100 percent leveraged.

Lien An encumbrance against a property for tax or other reasons that restricts the freedom to dispose of it until the encumbrance is removed or satisfied.

Listing An agreement between the owner of property and a real estate agent for the offering of the property for sale or rent.

Loan constant The regular monthly or annual payment due on a mortgage over the life of the loan.

Loan-to-value ratio A percentage of the estimated value of property that a lending institution is willing to provide to finance real estate.

Long-term financing A mortgage for a period of years that is secured by real estate.

Market approach The most reliable indication of value of real estate, based on a comparison of a property with other properties of the same type that have recently sold in the open market.

Market rent The amount of rent that the market has proved willing to accept for a specific size and type of property.

Market value The amount that a knowledgeable buyer would pay and a knowledgeable seller would accept for a property after it has been on the market for a sufficient period to test its attractiveness to potential buyers.

Mortgage A document stating the agreement of a lender to provide funds to a borrower who agrees to repay that amount on terms defined in the document. Real estate serves as the collateral for the loan.

Mortgagee The lender to whom real estate is pledged as security for a loan.

Mortgagor The borrower who pledges real estate to a lender as security for a loan.

Multiple listing An agreement among brokers whereby property listed for sale by one may also be sold by other parties to the agreement.

Net income The income remaining after reduction of gross income by operating expenses and a provision for vacancy and collection loss, but before debt service or depreciation for tax purposes.

Note An instrument in which one party agrees to pay to another a specified amount by a specified time.

Open listing A nonexclusive sales agreement in which any number of agents are given an opportunity to sell a property with the commission being paid to the one who delivers a purchaser or renter.

Operating expenses All expenses of owning a property except interest, mortgage amortization, depreciation, and real estate taxes.

Operating income All income actually provided by a property except tax shelter.

Option The right given for a consideration to purchase or lease a property under specified terms for a specified period of time.

GLOSSARY

Overimprovement An improvement that is excessive in terms of its relationship to the value of the property or to the eventual return on the property.

Permanent loan A long-term loan that usually replaces a shorter-term loan that involved payment for construction or rehabilitation.

Points A percentage of the total loan amount that is paid as a fee to the lender to make the loan by increasing the lender's yield.

Principal The total amount borrowed or the amount remaining to be paid back to a lender.

Prepayment penalty A payment exacted from the borrower by the lender when a mortgage loan is paid off before its term is up, usually a percentage of the loan balance.

Realtor® A real estate broker or sales agent who is affiliated with the National Association of Realtors®.

Refinance Restructuring or renegotiating financing to obtain better terms or a greater sum of money. Usually involves paying off an existing loan and establishing a new one.

Return The amount realized after recapture of the original investment in a property.

Secondary financing Financing of real estate by a party whose claim to the collateral comes second to that of the first-mortgage holder.

Second mortgage An additional loan beyond the first mortgage with second priority in case of a default.

Short-term loan A short-duration loan, usually 3 years or less, that is used to pay for construction and other expenses of rehabilitation.

Straight-line depreciation The accounting procedure that assumes an equal amount of annual depreciation over an economic life allowed by the government.

Subcontractor A skilled tradesperson who performs construction work for individuals or general contractors.

Subordinate An acknowledgment that a debt is inferior to the debt of another creditor.

Tax shelter A reduction in current tax obligations by taking allowable deductions from real estate to offset taxable income.

Term The specified duration of a loan or lease.

Title A legal document indicating lawful ownership of specified land.

Underimprovement An improvement that does not contribute its proportionate share to the value of a property.

Underwrite A decision as to whether to make a mortgage loan and in what amount, based on the borrower's ability to repay the loan and on the collateral offered by the applicant for a loan.

Yield The return on investment, including the gain over the original equity commitment, that is earned when the property is sold.

Zoning Rules and regulations concerning the allowable uses of land in an area, such as a village or township.

Index

Accelerated depreciation, definition, 169
Accountants:
  advice from, 144, 159
  fees of, 39, 144
  role in financing, 63, 64
Administrative costs, 33–34, 41
Advertising:
  bulletin board, 149, 158
  costs of, 149
    allocation of, 33, 34, 39
  free, 136, 149, 158
  newspaper, 136, 149, 158
  for property wanted, 13
  for tenants, 136
  wording of, 136–137
Aesthetic considerations, 3–4, 113
  color, use of, 113–114, 120
Agents, real estate (*see* Real estate brokers)
Agreement of sale, definition, 169
Air conditioning, 26, 116, 117
  common areas, 148
  cost estimating, 22, 34
  through heating plant, 126, 127
  room size units, 22, 127
Air traffic noise, 11
Amenity, definition, 169
Amortization, definition, 169
Amortization tables, use of, 45
Appliances, kitchen, 21, 109, 117, 119
Appraisal:
  capitalization approach, 47
  cost approach, 170
  definition, 169
  frequency of, 38
  prerehabilitation, 80
Appraisers, inspection by, 24–26
Appreciation of property, 2, 46, 151
  definition, 169
Architects:
  fees of, 25, 33, 96, 97
  as general contractors, 96–97
  as inspectors, 24–25
  selection of, 96

Architectural drawings, 96
Asking price, 49, 52
Assessed value:
  appealing, 143
  definition, 169
  previous assessments, record of, 27–28
Assessments, condominium, 166
Assumption of mortgage (*see* Mortgages, assumption of)
Attics:
  insulation, 129
  storage, 125
Attorneys, 54, 158, 159
  fees of, 33, 34, 144
Auditing fees, allocation of, 33, 34
Automobile expenses, 39, 148

Balance sheet, definition, 169
Balloon payment, definition, 169
Basements:
  dryness, 19–20
  finishing, 79, 100, 101, 133
  recreation area, 116
  storage in, 125
Bathrooms:
  addition, 121, 122
  division, 122
  evaluation, 21–22
  inspection, official, 101
  modernization, 78, 109, 120–123
  number, 116, 121
  painting of, 110
  ventilation, 22, 101
Bathtubs, 110, 123
Bedrooms, number of, 116
Benches, backyard, 107
Blinds, window, 111
Boiler explosion insurance, 38, 40
Boilers, 26, 147
  installation, 100
Breezeways, 100
Brokers (*see* Real estate brokers)

175

176 | INDEX

Building code, 101–102
  definition, 169
  inspection for violations of, 27
  loan to correct violations of, 71
Building engineers, 145
Building inspection (*see* Inspection of buildings)
Building inspector's office, records of, 27
Building permits (*see* Permits)
Bulletin board advertising, 149, 158
Burglar alarms, 37
Buyers:
  checking out, 157
  condominium, 165–166
Buyers' market, negotiating in, 53

Cabinets:
  kitchen, 109, 117–119
  medicine, 109
Capital gain, definition, 169
Capital improvement, definition, 169
Capitalization process, 43
  appraisal, 47
  definition, 170
  income approach, definition, 171
Capitalization rate, 48–49, 153
  definition, 170
Carpentry, 40, 118
Carpets, 40, 108, 113
Carports, storage in, 125
Cash flow (*see* Net income)
Caulking:
  bathroom, 123
  insulating effect, 130
Ceilings, 113
  illustration, 114
Cesspools, 16
Changing neighborhood (*see* Neighborhood evaluation)
Charge accounts with suppliers, 75
Children of tenants, 12, 116
  fencing for, 105
Chimneys:
  erection, 100
  inspection, 16, 26
Cleaning expenses, 36, 40
Closets, 117, 125
Closing costs, 65
  definition, 170
Collateral, definition, 170
Color, use of, 113–114, 120
Commercial activity in neighborhoods, 10
Commissions, broker, 13, 39, 64, 138, 157
  definition, 170
Comparable sales, definition, 170
Concessions, negotiating:
  nonprice, 55
  price, 54–55
Conditional contract, definition, 170

Condominiums, conversion to, 2, 161–167
  definition, 170
  grounds for, 162–164
  negative indications, 164–165
  restrictions, 165
  second mortgage offer, 166
  unit pricing, 166
Constant, mortgage payment, definition, 170
Construction in area, 11
Construction loans, definition, 170
Contract sale, definition, 170
Contractors:
  arbitration of disagreements with, 95
  changes during course of work, discussion concerning, 95
  contract with, 92–93, 95–96
  definition, 170
  direct payment by lender, 80, 95
  as factor in choice of type of building, 3
  garage specialists, 132
  general, definition, 171
  inspection by, 24, 25
  insurance coverage of, 93, 94
  "licensed," 102
  lien, waiver of, obtained from, 93
  nonperformance clause for termination of, 96
  permits obtained by, 93
  purchasing by, 93–94
  rates and fees of, 25, 95
  registration of investor as, 102
  scheduling of work by, 92
  selection of, 93–94
  self as, 91–92
  specifications given to, 93, 95
  working relations with, 94–95
  (*See also* Subcontractors)
Conversion:
  to condominiums (*see* Condominiums, conversion to)
  definition, 170
  single to multiple unit, 100
Cosmetic improvements:
  exterior, 105–107
  interior, 107–114
  return as criterion for, 104
Cost approach, definition, 170
Costs:
  cosmetic repairs and, 104
  estimating, 77
  maximum, 49
  spread sheet of, 141–142
  of utilities, tenant payment of, 127–128
  (*See also specific costs, for example:* Administrative costs; Advertising, costs of)
Counters, kitchen, 119
Couples as tenants, 115–116
Credit:
  establishing, 77–78
  limitations on, 7

Credit unions, 75
Crime in neighborhood, 10, 11
   urban renewal and, 69–70, 72
"Curb appeal," 106

Debt service, definition, 170
Deed, definition, 170
Deferred maintenance, definition, 170
Dehumidifiers, 125
Dens, 116
Deposits:
   by investors, 53, 55
   security, 149
Depreciation:
   accelerated, definition, 169
   definition, 170–171
   straight-line, definition, 173
Dishwashers, 115, 116, 118
Doors:
   closing devices, 147
   front, attractiveness of, 106, 107
   inspection, 16
   insulation, 146–147
   sliding, 124
   storm, 129–131
Down payments, 7, 60–64
   conventional mortgage percentage, 73
   land contract, 65–68
   life insurance loans, 61
   partners as source of, 62
   private loans, 61–62
   refinancing, 6, 61
   rehabilitation costs and, 60
   second mortgage as source, 7
   seller as source, 63–64
   size, 59, 60
Downs, Anthony, 9
Draperies, 40, 112
Driveways, 100
Dryers, clothes (*see* Washers and dryers)

Easements, 28
   definition, 171
Economic life of building, definition, 171
Effective age of building, definition, 171
Effective income (*see* Net income)
Electric costs, 34, 39, 146
   individual meters, 127
Electrical systems, 26, 28
   conformance to National Electrical Code, 120
   government requirements, 100–101
   installation or alteration, 100–101, 119–120, 123
Elevators, 40
Emergency repairs, 141, 146
Engineering fees, allocation of, 33
Engineers, building, 145

Entertainment in neighborhood, 12
Entryways, 107–109, 111–112
Equity, definition, 171
Escrow, definition, 171
Estimates, cost, 77
Evaluation (*see* Inspection of buildings; Neighborhood evaluation)
Eviction of tenants, 102
Exchange of property, 154–155
Exclusive listing, definition, 171
Exhaust fans, 22, 120, 125
Experience of seller as negotiating factor, 52
Experts:
   advice of, 77
   inspection by, 14, 24–27
Exterior of building, 37, 105–107
Exterminating costs, 35, 40, 146, 148

Failure of negotiations, 56
Falstein, Richard, 3–4, 5
Family composition, 115–117
Fans, exhaust, 22, 120, 125
Faucets, 123
Federal Housing Administration (FHA), 71, 74
Fees, 33, 34, 39
   (*See also specific fees, for example:* Architects, fees of; Auditing fees, allocation of)
Fences, 100, 105, 106
FHA (Federal Housing Administration), 71, 74
Field, Jerry, 105, 111
Financing, 59–86
   accountant role in, 63, 64
   down payment (*see* Down payments)
   Federal Housing Administration as information source, 71
   government, 68–72
   interim, definition, 171
   land contract, 65–58
   long-term, definition, 172
   mortgages (*see* Mortgages)
   negotiating, 72–81
   occupancy as factor, 5
   refinancing (*see* Refinancing)
   rehabilitation (*see* Property improvement loans)
   secondary, definition, 173
   Section 312 program, 70–72
   by seller, 63–65, 84
   type of building and, 4–5
   (*See also* Loans)
Fire code compliance, 36
Fire insurance, 38, 40
Fireplaces, 26
First mortgage, definition, 171
   (*See also* Mortgages)
Flooding, 11

178 | INDEX

Floor plans, 27, 125
   kitchen, 101, 118–119
Floors:
   condition of, 20, 79
   sanding, 108
Fluorescent lighting, 120, 147
Foreclosure, definition, 171
Foundations, building, 16, 26–27
Fuel costs:
   estimating, 34, 35, 40
   minimizing, 35, 146
   tenant payment of, 125–126, 146
Furnaces (*see* Heating plants)

Game facilities, 107
Garages:
   addition or expansion, 131–132
   building, 100
   rental, 31
   storage in, 125
Garbage removal, 35, 40, 148
Gas costs:
   control of, 146
   estimating, 34, 35, 39, 40
   tenant payment of, 146
Gas and electric companies, 127
General contractors (*see* Contractors)
Government financing, 68–72
Government records, inspection of, 27–28
Government services, 10, 11, 14
Gross income, 31–32, 44
   definition, 171
Gross operating income, 31–32
Grounds:
   inspection of, 16
   maintenance of, 37, 40, 148, 149
   use of, 107, 116–117
   (*See also* Landscaping)
Guest rooms, 116
Gutted building, choice of, 3
Gutters, 16

Halls, 107–109, 111–112
Hardware maintenance, 40
Hardware stores, 87, 90–91
Heat:
   common areas, 126, 148
   costs of, 35, 146
      estimating, 34, 35, 40
      tenant payment of, 125–126, 146
Heating plants, 125–127
   fuel (*see* Fuel costs)
   inspection, 26, 28
   installing or extending, 100, 126–127
Heir as seller, 52
Holding property after rehabilitation, 152–154

Homeowner's policy, 93, 171
Hot water heaters (*see* Boilers)

Improvements:
   priorities in, 109
   (*See also* Cosmetic improvements)
Income:
   estimating, 29, 31–33, 44
   gross, 31–32, 44, 171
   market value and, 29
   net (*see* Net income)
   operating (*see* Operating income)
Income approach, definition, 171
Income/Expense Analysis (Institute of Real Estate Management), 41
Income and expense statement, 46, 171
Income-producing property, definition, 171
Inflation:
   asking price and, 52
   minimizing, through cost payments by tenants, 128
Inspection of buildings, 13, 15–27, 101–102
   checklist, 16–17
   evaluation of exterior, 16–17
   by expert, 14, 24–27
   variety of buildings, importance of seeing, 29
Installment sale, 156–157
   definition, 171
Institute of Real Estate Management:
   Income/Expense Analysis, 41
   operating statements, recommended form for, 33
Insulation, 19, 128–131, 146–147
Insurance:
   contractors covered by, 93, 94
   costs of, 38, 40, 41, 143
   coverage-claim ratios, 143–144
   homeowner's, 93, 171
   liability, 38, 40, 93, 143, 144
   life, 61, 75
   subcontractors, coverage of, 93
Interest:
   amortization tables, use to determine, 45
   mortgage, 62, 82–84, 142
   private loans, 61–62
   refinancing and, 61
   second mortgage, 62
   term of loan and, 4, 171
Interim financing, definition, 171
Interior of building, 107–114
Interior designers, 4
Investments:
   alternate, 59–60, 156
   previous real estate, credit and, 78

Janitor service costs, 1–2, 39, 41
   snow removal, 36–37, 148, 149

# INDEX

Job history and credit, 77, 78
Junior mortgages, definition, 171

Kaplan, Richard, 9
Kitchens:
  appliances, 21, 109, 117, 119
  evaluation, 20–21
  layout, 101, 116, 118–120
  modernization, 78, 109, 117–120
  storage in, 21, 109, 117–119
  tenant type and, 115–117

Labor:
  paid, 24, 88
    contractor (*see* Contractors)
    janitorial, 1–2, 39, 41
  unpaid, 2, 87–91
Land, value of, 48
Land contracts, 65–68
Landscaping, 40, 79, 148–149
Laundry equipment (*see* Washers and dryers)
Lavatories (*see* Bathrooms)
Lawn maintenance, 37, 40, 148, 149
Layout (*see* Floor plans)
Leases, 103, 139–140
  definition, 171
Legal fees, 33, 34, 144
Lessee:
  definition, 172
  (*See also* Tenants)
Lessor, definition, 172
Leverage, 59–60, 81
  definitions, 84, 172
Liability insurance, 38, 40, 93, 143, 144
Licenses (*see* Permits)
Liens:
  definition, 172
  waiver from contractor, 93
Life insurance loans, 61, 75
Lighting:
  costs of, 36, 37, 147
  exterior, 106, 147, 148
  fluorescent, 120, 147
  interior, 108–109, 147, 148
Listing cards, 13–15
Listing of property:
  exclusive, definition, 171
  multiple, definition, 172
  open, definition, 172
Loan constant, definition, 172
Loan-to-value ratio, definition, 172
Loans:
  to correct violations of building codes, 71
  (*See also* Financing; *specific loans, for example:* Construction loans; Private loans)
Locks, 37
Logan, Robert L., 94
Long-term financing, definition, 172

Maintenance:
  costs of, 36–38, 41
  deferred, 170
  grounds, 37, 40, 148, 149
  tenant morale and, 140
  by tenants, 5, 136
Management costs, 144–145
Margin, lender's, 59
Market approach, definition, 172
Market rent, 14
  definition, 172
Market value, 29, 47–49
  definition, 172
Masonry repairs, 100
Materials, cost estimates for, 24
Medicine cabinets, 109
Merchants, information from, 11
Meters, individual, 19
Mirrors, 109
Monthly assessments, condominium, 166
Mortgages:
  assumption of, 53, 64–65
    definition, 169
    refusal to permit, 66
  condominium, 165–166
  constant payment, definition, 170
  conventional, 73
  definition, 172
  first, definition, 171
  junior, definition, 171
  maximum, rule-of-thumb for, 7
  mortgagee, 156, 157
    definition, 172
  mortgagor, definition, 172
  neighborhood and, 10
  payments:
    constant, 170
    interest, 62, 82–84, 142
    net income and, 44
    prepayment penalties, 74, 173
    principal, 142, 173
    spread sheet, 142
    variable, 46
  permanent, definition, 173
  principal, 142, 173
  prior, records of, 28
  rates, 6, 46, 170
  second (*see* Second mortgages)
  Section 312 program, 70–72
  term of, 67
  variable, 46
Motor vehicle expenses, 39, 148
Moving buildings, 100
Multiple listing, definition, 172
Municipal governments, programs administered by, 70

National Association of Realtors, 173
Negotiating process, 51–58

180 INDEX

Neighborhood evaluation, 5, 9–28, 30, 32
  checklist, 14
  condominium conversion and, 162
  rehabilitation, present, 14, 68–70
  resale and, 153, 156
Neighborhood Housing Services (NHS), 69
Neighborhood organization, value of, 10
Net income:
  balance sheet, 169
  cash flow defined as, 170
  definition, 171
  determination of, 32, 33, 42–44, 150–154
    checklist, 42–43
  increasing, 128–129, 151, 154
  market value and, 47
  and occupancy by owner, 44–45
  resale price and, 152–153
Net operating income, 32–33
Newspapers, choice of, 136, 149, 158
NHS (Neighborhood Housing Services), 69
Nonperformance clauses, 95
Norton, Don, 140
Note, definition, 172
Nuisances, neighborhood, 11, 14

Occupancy by owner, 1, 2, 5, 14
  government requirements, 68, 72
  net income and, 44–45
Offer to buy, 53–54
Office expenses, 33, 39
Oil heat, 126–127
  (*See also* Fuel costs)
Open listing, definition, 172
Operating expenses, 34–38
  checklist, 39–41
  definition, 172
  estimating, 29, 32–33
  insurance, 38
  taxes, 37–38
Operating income, 29, 33
  definition, 172
  gross, 31–32
  net, 32–33
Overassessment, appearing, 143
Overimprovement, definition, 173
Owner occupancy (*see* Occupancy by owner)
Ownership:
  absentee, 10, 14
  multiple, offer to buy and, 55
  term of, 81

Painting:
  of bathrooms, 110
  color selection, 113
  costs of, 36, 39–40, 106
  exterior, 105–107
  staining compared with, 105, 111
Paneling, 79
  ceiling, illustration, 113–114

Parking facilities, 12, 40
Partners:
  advantages of, 88
  brokers as source of, 63
  and yield, 62, 63
Paved areas, 16
Payroll expenses, 39, 41
Permanent loan, definition, 173
Permits, 10, 39, 99–101
  contractor obtains, 93
  issuance of, inspection before, 27
  prior, record of, 28
Pets, fences for, 105
Pipes, insulation of, 147
Plans:
  changes in, cost of, 95
  permit applications and, 101
Plastic, laminated, 119
Play equipment, 107
Play space, 116
Plumbing:
  construction or alteration of, 100, 101, 118
  inspection of, 26, 101
  insulation of, 147
  testing, 20
Plumbing materials, durability of, 26
Points (mortgage), definition, 173
Police protection, 10, 69, 70
Porches, 100
Prepayment penalties, 74
  definition, 173
Pricing, 159, 167
  negotiating concessions in, 54–55
Principal, 142
  definition, 173
Profit (*see* Yield)
Property improvement loans, 74–77, 79
  interest, 79–80
  payment, 80
Property taxes, 40, 142–143
Purchase decision, 46–50

Raising buildings, 100
Real estate brokers:
  commissions of, 13, 39, 64, 138, 157, 170
  employees of, 15–16
  exchange of property and, 155
  exclusive listing, definition, 171
  as go-betweens, 53–54, 158
  multiple listing, definition, 172
  open listing, definition, 172
  pressure by, 53
  Realtor, definition, 173
  rivalry between, 57
  as source of partners, 63
  tenant acquisition through, 138
  viewing appointments made by, 18
Real estate taxes, 40
Real income (*see* Net income)
Realtor (*see* Real estate broker)

… INDEX 181

Records:
  government, 27–28
  importance of, 114
  spread sheet, 141–142
Recreation rooms, 116
Redlining, 73
References, personal, 138, 157
Refinancing, 6, 61, 153–154
  definition, 173
Refrigerators, 109, 117, 119
Rental income (*see* Rents)
Rental procedures, 135–150
  (*See also* Leases)
Rents:
  collection, 149–150
  economic, definition, 171
  estimating, 30–32, 43–44
  excessive, 137–138
  garages as source of, 131–132
  gross operating income and, 31–32
  market, 14, 172
  and number of units, 2
  reduction for janitorial service, 136
  schedules, 31
  utilities and, 126–128
  vacancy losses, 30–32
Repairs, 36, 140, 145–146
  emergency, 141, 146
Replacement reserve, 41–42
Residents of neighborhood, 11
Restaurants, accessibility of, 12
Retainers (repairmen), 145
Return on investment (*see* Yield)
Risk, degree of, 4–5
Rooms, size of, 79, 124
Rubbish removal, 10, 35, 40, 148

Safety of neighborhood (*see* Security)
Sale and leaseback, 6–7
Sanitation service, 10, 35, 40, 148
Scheduling workmen, 89, 92
Scherer, Frank, 91
Schools, quality of, 11–12
Second mortgages, 7, 64–65
  condominium buyer, 166
  definition, 173
  holding, 156
  rates, 62
Secondary financing, definition, 173
Section 312 program, 70–72
Security, 5, 137
  costs of, 37, 40
  in urban renewal areas, 69–70, 72
Security deposits, 149
Selection of property, 3, 9–28
Seller, 51–54, 158
  financing by, 63–65, 84
Seller's market, negotiating in, 53
Selling property after rehabilitation, 151–159
Septic tanks, 16

Service costs, 41
Sewer costs, 34, 35, 39, 148
Shades, window, 112
Shopping facilities, 12
Shoring buildings, 100
Short-term loan, definition, 173
Showers, 20, 123
Showing property, 137
Shutters, window, 106
Siding, building, 100, 106
Single-family houses, 136
Single tenants, 116–117
Sinks, 21, 118, 123
Size of building, break-even, 2
Snow removal, 36–37, 148, 149
Soundproofing, 20
Spread sheet, 141–142
Staining, painting compared with, 105, 111
Stairways, 112
Storage space, 21, 109, 117–119, 125
Storm windows and doors, 16, 129–131
Stoves, 109, 117, 119
Straight-line depreciation, definition, 173
Strunk, Norman, 79
Subcontractors, 91–93
  definition, 173
Subordinate debt, definition, 173
Supplies, cost of, 35
Swings, backyard, 107

Tax assessor's office, records of, 27–28
Tax returns as selling aid, 158
Tax shelter, definition, 173
Tax stamps, 28, 52
Taxes:
  deductions, 122
  deferred, definition, 170
  depreciation and, definition, 170–171
  estimating, 37–38, 40, 41
  exchange of property and, 154–155
  installment sale and, 156
  payroll, 41
  property, 40, 142–143
  purchase decision and, 46
  real estate, 40
  sale and leaseback and, 7
  sale of property and, 152, 156
Technical skills, 87, 89–90
  credit availability and, 78
Telephone costs, 39
Television master antenna, 40
Tenants, 135–150
  advertising for, 136
  checking prospective, 138–139
  children of, 12, 105, 116
  color selection by, 114
  condominium conversion and, 161–162
  investor viewing appointments and, 18
  leases and, 103
  lessee, definition, 172

Tenants *(Cont.):*
  maintenance by, 5, 136
  present, 103–104, 135, 137, 138
  selection of, 135–140
  showing property to prospective, 137
  types of, 115–117
  utility payments by, 127–128
Term (time measure), definition, 173
Theft in neighborhood, 70, 107
  (*See also* Security)
Tile, bathroom, 110, 123
Timing of sale, 55
Title, definition, 173
Toilets, 123
Transportation:
  availability of, 12
  costs of, 148
Trash removal, 10, 35, 40, 148
Tuckpointing, 106
Turnover, tenant, 32

Underimprovement, definition, 173
Underwriting, definition, 173
Units, optimum number of, 100
Urban renewal, 68–72

Vacancies, apartment, 18, 30–32
Value-enhancing projects, 78
Vandalism in neighborhood, 70
Vending machines, 31
Ventilation systems, 22, 100, 101

Wallpaper, 109–110
Walls, 124–125
  insulation, 129

Washers and dryers, 116, 117
  coin-operated, 31
  cost of providing, 39, 40
  installation, 131, 133
Water costs:
  estimating, 34, 35, 39
  reduction of, 35, 146
Water heaters (*see* Boilers)
Weatherstripping, 130–131, 147
White, William, 97
Window guards, 37
Window washing, 35
Windows:
  appearance, 107, 111–112
  blinds and shades, 111–112
  in common areas, 111–112
  draperies, 40, 111–112
  inspection, 16, 20
  insulation, 16, 129–131, 146–147
  refinishing frames, 111
  replacement, 130
  storm, 16, 129–131
  thermal, 130
Wood surfaces, finishing, 105, 111
Workers' compensation insurance, 38, 40
Working couples, 115–116
Workmen, scheduling, 89, 92

Yards (*see* Grounds)
Yield:
  definition, 17
  estimating, 43
  partners and, 62, 63
  tax benefits and building appreciation, 43, 157

Zoning, 13, 28
  definition, 173
  variance application, 100